50 THINGS
TO SEE AND DO IN
NORTHERN NEW MEXICO'S
ENCHANTED
CIRCLE

MARK D. WILLIAMS &
AMY BECKER WILLIAMS

WESTWINDS
PRESS®

Text and photos © 2018 by Mark D. Williams and Amy Becker Williams

All rights reserved. No part of this book may be reproduced, stored in a retrieval system, or transmitted in any form or by any means, electronic, mechanical, photocopying, recording, or otherwise, without written permission from the publisher.

Library of Congress Control Number: 2018943828

ISBN 9781513261287 (paperback)
ISBN 9781513261294 (hardbound)
ISBN 9781513261300 (e-book)

Edited by Michelle Blair and Olivia Ngai
Indexed by Sheila Ryan
Overview Map by Betsy Beier

WestWinds Press®
An imprint of

GraphicArtsBooks.com

GRAPHIC ARTS BOOKS
Publishing Director: Jennifer Newens
Marketing Manager: Angela Zbornik
Editor: Olivia Ngai
Design & Production: Rachel Lopez Metzger

CONTENTS

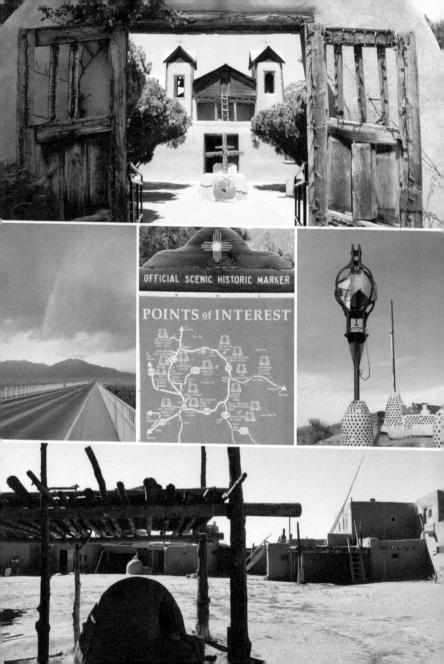

INTRODUCTION

Both of our families have been coming to the Enchanted Circle since we were kids. As a couple, we've been coming here for the last twenty-five years and have a second home in Taos; we love this part of the world that much. We have traveled together all over the world but keep coming back to the Southwest, keep coming back to the Enchanted Circle.

We are both teachers (Mark for high school, and Amy for elementary) and we will each be retiring soon. We chose Taos as our retirement home. The climate is great, the food sublime, the fishing and outdoor recreation top notch, the skiing world class, and the people friendly and interesting. The Enchanted Circle has great craft brews and award-winning wineries, unique shopping, an interesting mixture of so many cultures that produced this weird, cool, awesome culture of clothing, cuisine, rugs, sculpture, paintings, literature, and so much more. From Taos, we are close to the Colorado border; close to Santa Fe and Las Vegas, New Mexico; close to Texas. We are also close to several ski resorts, dozens of trout streams, hundreds of miles of hiking trails, and, of course, we are close to some of the finest restaurants in the Southwest.

The Enchanted Circle is a unique result of history and geography. The region enjoys a rich tapestry of peoples and culture. Tourism is the driving economic force for the Enchanted Circle's communities today and they see up to a million visitors annually. We enjoy and love the region so much, have explored so many of its secrets and joys, that we felt obliged and honored to share it with you.

From left to right, top: El Santuario de Chimayó. Middle: Rio Grande Gorge Bridge; Official Scenic Historic Marker; Earthships. Bottom: Taos Pueblo.

New Mexico's
ENCHANTED CIRCLE

RIO GRANDE
GORGE BRIDGE

Chimayó

Santa Fe ↙

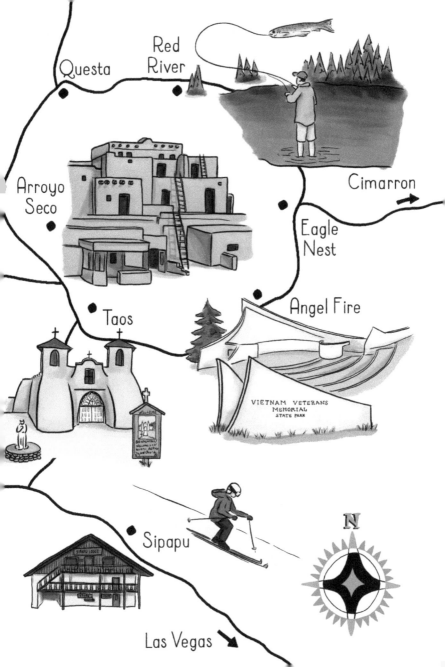

GETTING TO TAOS & THE ENCHANTED CIRCLE

Generally there are two primary routes to get to the Enchanted Circle: 1) from the southwest (Albuquerque or Santa Fe) or 2) from the east, hitting Cimarron into Eagle Nest. If you are coming from Santa Fe for a day trip or longer, you can take the High Road or the Low Road to reach the Enchanted Circle. Which is better? We like going up the High, coming back the Low. The other main entry into the Enchanted Circle is through Cimarron and Eagle Nest on the eastern side of the byway. You cut off on NM 58 west to US 64 west at Cimarron then on to Eagle Nest.

Cities near Taos and the Mileage to the Enchanted Circle Starting at Taos Plaza

From Albuquerque: 135 miles, 2.5 hours. I-25 north to Santa Fe; exit on NM 599 north to bypass Santa Fe; US 285 north to NM 68 north to Taos.

From Breckenridge: 263 miles, 4 hours. CO 9 south to Fairplay; US 285 south and CO 17 south to Alamosa; US 285 south to Tres Piedras; US 64 east to Taos.

From Crested Butte: 271 miles, 4.5 hours. CO 135 south to Gunnison; US 50 east to US 285 south to CO 17 south to Alamosa; US 285 south to Tres Piedras; US 64 east to Taos.

From Denver: 300 miles, 4.5 hours. I-25 south to Colorado Springs to Walsenburg; US 160 west to Fort Garland; CO 159 south and NM 522 south to Taos.

From Durango: 208 miles, 3.25 hours. US 160 east to Pagosa Springs; US 84 east to Chama; CO 17 south to Antonito; US 285 south to Tres Piedras; US 64 east to Taos.

From Vail: 276 miles, 4.5 hours. I-70 east to Copper Mountain; CO 91 south to Leadville; US 24 east and CO 17 south to Alamosa; US 285 south to Tres Piedras; US 64 east to Taos.

From Amarillo: 302 miles, 4.5 hours. I-40 west to Clines Corners; US 285 north to I-25 south to Santa Fe; US 84/285 to NM 68 north to Taos.

–from taos.org/plan-your-trip/getting-around/

THE ENCHANTED CIRCLE MILE BY MILE

This mile-by-mile chart is to be used as you plan your driving trip around the Enchanted Circle starting with Taos Plaza intersection as your genesis. Set your mileage counter at zero and you'll be able follow the chart along your route.

Ground Zero TAOS PLAZA intersection

0.1 Kit Carson Park

0.5 Split to Taos Pueblo on the right, but stay left (north) on NM 522

1.2 Taos Pueblo entrance right (east) on Hail Creek Road. This is a second entrance to the Taos Pueblo. You'll see the smoke shop just off the road to your left when you turn.

2.1 Historical marker (Taos history) on right with pullout

2.4 Overland Ranch complex

3.9 Cutoff to Arroyo Seco and Taos Ski Valley right (east) on NM 150

4.0 Four-way light (the Old Blinking Light). Turn left (west) on US 64 to Rio Grande Gorge and Earthships, north on NM 522 to Questa.

5.3 Historical marker (Taos/Gorge) on left

10.5 Cross the bridge over Rio Hondo and turn left (west) on B006 and, after a bit, B007 to go to John Dunn Bridge over Rio Grande; here you start your climb to Questa (the road keeps climbing for a good ways).

Scrub oak, juniper, sage, mountains to your right.

13.8 Historical marker (D.H. Lawrence Ranch) and entrance on the right to D.H. Lawrence Ranch

14.5 San Cristobal

Still climbing (piñon and juniper).

17.3 Garrapata Canyon

17.9 Cebolla Mesa (left) includes parking area

20.0 Red River Hatchery turnoff (turn left or west on NM 515 for 2 miles)

21.3	The valley opens up in front of you and you can see the edge of Questa.
21.9	"Questa Welcomes You" sign
22.5	Crossing bridge over Red River
23.7	Traffic light. To get to Red River, turn right (east) on NM 38 and follow for winding 12 miles ahead.
24.0	Historical marker (Cienega) on the right

Note you are leaving scrub oak and seeing more pine trees.

25.2	Eagle Rock Lake Day Use Area (right)
25.5	Red River to the right
27.1	Goat Hill Campground (Molycorp Mine begins to your left)

Watch for bighorn sheep and retaining walls and slides here and there.

| 28.7 | Columbine Creek Canyon Hike (right) |

Curvy road past aspens and pines.

30.3	Molycorp Mine in full view to your left
31.8	Ascent and curves; La Bobita Campground (left)
32.8	Elephant Rock Campground (left); recent slide near
33.2	Fawn Lakes Campground
33.9	June Bug Campground
34.2	Historical marker (Red River Valley) on right

You are on edge of the town of Red River.

35.0	Welcome to Red River. Slow down.
35.8	Red River Community House
37.0	Road splits. Go left (east) on NM 38 to Bobcat Pass and Eagle Nest (to continue on Enchanted Circle); curvy high mountain road; right (southeast) on NM 578 goes to upper Red River for alpine sightseeing, headwaters fishing.
38.7	Enchanted Forest Cross Country Ski Area (MM16)
39.2	Bobcat Pass (9,820 feet)

You are going downhill now. Don't ride your brakes. Shift to lower gears.

| 47.1 | Elizabethtown on the right. You will see a weathered "Gold Rush Days" sign to your left. The ghost town is across the road to your right. |

Now you'll drop down even more and pass fewer aspens.

You'll start to see the edge of the Eagle Nest community.

50.9 Welcome to Eagle Nest. Stop and enjoy here; perhaps visit Cimarron (US 64 E) as a nice side trip. You reach the Cimarron River in about a mile and will drive 24 miles east along the river to get to the village of Cimarron. Those 24 miles are winding and the speed limit low so it takes at least 35 to 40 minutes.

51.9 Passing NM 38/US 64 intersection

53.2 Eagle Nest Lake State Park entrance

55.4 Pullout for Wheeler Peak in the distance

56.9 Day use area

60.4 Vietnam Veterans Memorial State Park

61.2 NM 434. Angel Fire (8,420 feet) to your left (east)

   0.0 Turn left on NM 434

   0.7 Angel Fire Airport

   2.6 Entrance to resort (left) and visitors center (right)

62.6 Elliot Barker Trail 1

64.4 Palo Flechado Pass

Coming down, you'll enter Taos Canyon.

69.5 Valle Escondido

74.6 Shady Brook

75.0 La Sombra Day Use Area

78.2 Historical Marker (Taos Canyon) on the right

79.6 Devisadero Trail and South Boundary Trails off to the left and "Welcome to Taos" sign to the right

80.0 Split intersection. Take a right (north) on NM 68, 3 miles to Taos Plaza

THE ENCHANTED CIRCLE

Distance: 84 miles, 2.5 to 3 hours if you drive with minimal stops. Plan on a full day if you stop in each town and to take pictures.

Route: From Taos Plaza, US 64 north to NM 522 north to Questa; NM 38 east to Red River, then continue on US 64 south to Eagle Nest and Angel Fire; US 64 west back to Taos.

Most visitors to the Enchanted Circle will come from Albuquerque and Santa Fe, and then go along the High Road or the Low Road. Here's the route of the Enchanted Circle: From Taos, take NM 522 North to Questa. At Questa, catch NM 38 east to Red River. Then go from Red River east to Elizabethtown continuing on NM 38, south to Eagle Nest. From Eagle Nest, head south on US 64 to Angel Fire. From Angel Fire, stay on US 64, back to Taos. The other main entry into the Enchanted Circle takes place through Cimarron and Eagle Nest on the eastern end of the byway. If you enter the Enchanted Circle from the east, you will cut off on NM 58 west to US 64 west at Cimarron then on to Eagle Nest. The trick is to choose your route and time wisely. Remember to be prepared for changing weather, especially during monsoon season from mid-July through September.

The Enchanted Circle is a spectacular 84-mile loop drive through mountains, mesa, great rifts, valleys and national forest, sprawling ranches, a gold-mining ghost town, cold clear streams, and a large unusual national monument. This US Scenic Byway hosts hundreds of thousands of visitors annually. The landscapes are varied and dramatic, unique to New Mexico. The diversity and beauty, grandeur and simplicity, sweeping vistas of mountains and of valleys—all in a circle—are breathtaking. Rarely will you find such differing landscapes, cultures, towns and villages, and lay of the land in such a small area.

From left to right, top: San Francisco de Asís Church; a sign of the Enchanted Circle; San José de Gracia Church. Middle: Rio Grande Gorge Bridge. Bottom: the state flag flying outside shops in Taos; religious mural in Chimayó.

The Rio Grande Gorge charms and awes its seekers.

The genesis of your drive around the Enchanted Circle will be dominated by a rift, a river, a range; to the west lies a ragged gash of earth, the Rio Grande Gorge, which divides the ancient volcanic cones from the snow-capped Sangre de Cristo Range to the east. The Enchanted Circle travels around New Mexico's largest mountain, Wheeler Peak, part of the Sangre de Cristo Mountain Range that spans from Southern Colorado to the southern parts of New Mexico. Steeped in history and raw beauty, this drive features expansive views, diverse landscapes, and frequent remnants of the Wild West.

This is a loop trip. You are driving in a circle. Easy as pie. Drive it, and you get a threefold reward: amazing scenery, a million things to do, and cool mountain villages. By cool, we mean the kind of cool a Popsicle provides in summer, and the type of cool that you wished you had when you watched Dean Martin and The Golddiggers on television. Each town has its own vibe, its own identity, its own charm.

This National Forest Scenic Byway circles Wheeler Peak, the highest point in New Mexico at 13,161 feet. Throughout the drive, you'll see some of the oldest rocks in the Southwest—quartz and feldspar that date back two billion years. You can view ancient petroglyphs, golden eagles, snow-capped peaks, historic sites, and Indian pueblos. Watch for special Enchanted Circle markers to help guide your way.

Exploring the Enchanted Circle Scenic Byway is a perfect way to spend an adventurous weekend or a week or two. The byway is only about 84 miles, but there is so much to see that you will want to take your time to see it all. As you drive out of Taos on NM 522, take a detour to see the Rio Grande Gorge Bridge, one of the highest bridges in America. Take a detour to the east so you can visit Arroyo Seco, a quaint artistic village on the road to the internationally flavored Taos Ski Valley.

As you continue north, you'll pass scenic Arroyo Hondo. After San Cristobal, visit the ranch where famous writer D.H. Lawrence lived. To the east, you will see the towering Sangre de Cristo Range. Passing Questa, you will encounter truly dramatic landscapes with access to the Rio Grande. A steep road to the east takes you to the mountain hamlet of Red River, which offers a spectacular vista of aspen and spruce groves.

Continue along the Enchanted Circle from NM 38 to US 64 through Eagle Nest Lake State Park with a spectacular 2,400-acre lake that's excellent for hiking, fishing, boating, and cross-country skiing. Watch for deer, elk, bear, and eagles. As you continue west, you will pass Angel Fire, another great family resort on the way back to Taos.

You can visit eight historical pueblos (Native American settlements) during your stay in northern New Mexico, the most famous of which is the Taos Pueblo. The nearby forested mountains abound in game: deer, elk, bear, and wild turkey. Seasonal trout fishing is outstanding in mountain lakes and streams and year-round in the Rio Grande. Try horseback riding through valleys surrounded by snow-capped peaks. Consider a raft trip down the Rio Grande River. Skiing and snowboarding may be enjoyed at several nearby resorts from Thanksgiving to Easter—Taos Ski Valley, Red River, Angel Fire, and Sipapu.

Opportunities for hiking and biking are plentiful on miles of developed trails in these areas offering dramatic vistas, wildlife viewing, solitude, and visits to prehistoric and historic cultural sites. There are hundreds of miles of trails, some maintained by volunteer groups. Opportunities also abound for hiking, horseback riding, mountain biking, and four-wheel-drive (4WD) exploring. Many summer hiking trails and forest roads become cross-country ski and snowmobile trails in winter.

HISTORY

This was wild country fully tamed only 120 years ago. Let that sink in. New Mexico only became a state in 1912. This region is still one of the wildest and most remote in the Southwest.

The history of northern New Mexico can be explained in waves. One wave of people came after another: the Pueblo Indians followed by Spanish, Anglo, Mexican, traders, Eastern Americans, artists and painters and writers, hippies and counter-culturalists. And the latest wave? Tourists from around the world. The nineteenth-century commercial highway Santa Fe Trail ran through this area, connecting the civilized world with the Wild West. Kit Carson, Bishop Jean-Baptiste Lamy, Father Jose Martinez, and other frontier heroes lived here, fought here, for varying reasons. Outlaws and famous Western personalities were a part of the historic fabric too, including Wyatt Earp, Jesse James, Buffalo Bill Cody, Annie Oakley, Billy the Kid. When horses and wagons were replaced by trains, the region continued to be a crossroads for trade and travelers.

The sign marking the historic San José de Gracia Church.

The history includes the Pueblo Indians, who lived under various rulers while trying to keep as much of their culture as they could. Once you visit the pueblos, you'll see that they were extraordinarily successful even through cultural intrusion and forcible control. First came the Spanish, then Mexican, and finally Americans. The Pueblo Indians eventually lived next to and with Anglos (sometimes) and Mexicans. We used to hear about how these three groups formed a tricultural community, but the area's population is more complex and varied than that simplified view would have you believe. The region's history saw revolts and reservations, barbed wire and cattle, six-shooters and bows and arrows, priests and outlaws, land grants and mining, bears and llamas, miners and hippies. Northern New Mexico is a melting pot of different cultures. Now, the region bends to tourism, with hundreds of thousands from around the world visiting each and every year, and it's only growing in numbers.

WEATHER

The region enjoys over three hundred days of sunshine a year and generally has a moderate climate, although it ranges from the dryness and heat of the high desert to the cool summers and bitter cold of the alpine mountains. The weather changes quickly here, so be prepared. In summer, it can be pleasantly cool in the morning, hot during lunch, rain and cooling in the afternoon, hot again before dinner, perfect temperature for outdoors eating by supper. In winter, you may see many bluebird days that reach into the fifties (degrees Fahrenheit), even sixties, but before you can blink, a snowstorm will have moved in and dumped a foot of snow. Again, be prepared.

July and August, the so-called monsoon season, are rainy months with almost daily afternoon showers. Make your plans accordingly. Mornings don't usually have as much rain as the afternoons. Visitors should carry rain gear. Daytime temperatures in the summer range from highs in the fifties to seventies in the higher elevations, and seventies to high eighties in the lower. Breaking ninety is not common,

Magical winter snowfall in Taos.

but it can happen. Many places have air conditioning, though you'll be surprised by how many do not. Adobe walls tend to keep temperatures inside cool and constant after all.

Temperatures can drop dramatically when a storm moves in. Nights are cool, worthy of a jacket, and by fall they're occasionally below freezing. Snowfall usually begins in early October. If you are hiking, beware of lightning on the ridges. Since you will probably be the highest point around, get off the ridge if thunderclouds are overhead.

Be sure to take proper clothing. Temperatures can drop suddenly in all seasons. Wet clothing can chill the body quickly. You can wear the space-age wicking materials, shells, or old-fashioned wool. But cotton next to the skin will keep the body damp and will actually wick heat away. That means jeans. Dress in layers that can be added or removed as the temperature changes.

Remember, the weather is sort of like the Enchanted Circle laid-back vibe. No hurry. You're on New Mexico time. Climate is perfect, and if it's not sunny at that moment, wait a few minutes; it will be soon.

DANGERS

ALTITUDE SICKNESS

Your body is not used to higher elevations, and if you try to do too much too soon, you'll likely suffer the effects of altitude sickness. Altitude sickness is a group of symptoms that range from headaches to vomiting.

The pressure of the air that surrounds you is called barometric pressure. When you venture into higher altitudes, this pressure drops and there is less oxygen available. Your body needs time to adjust to the change in pressure. There are three kinds of altitude sickness: acute mountain sickness (the mildest form), high-altitude pulmonary edema (a buildup of fluid in the lungs), and high-altitude cerebral edema (fluid in the brain).

Signs of altitude sickness:

- Headache
- Dizziness
- Nausea
- Vomiting
- Fatigue and loss of energy
- Shortness of breath
- Problems with sleep
- Less appetite

Symptoms usually show up within twelve to twenty-four hours of reaching these higher elevations. You typically get better within a day or two as your body adjusts to the change in altitude. If you get a headache and at least one other symptom associated with altitude sickness within a day or two of changing your elevation, you might have altitude sickness. Rest and drink lots of water; if your symptoms are more severe, you'll need medical attention.

The best way you can lower your chance of getting altitude sickness is through acclimatizing to the elevation slowly. Drink plenty of water, avoid alcohol and tobacco, and don't do much strenuous activity until the second day.

FROSTBITE

Frostbite is a serious condition where parts of your body actually freeze due to being not properly protected in frigid temperatures. Your extremities are at the biggest risk since they are further away from your warmer core. Frostnip, the first stage of frostbite, is when your unprotected skin gets red and sore. Take this signal as a serious warning to bundle up, get inside, and ward off progression to more serious stages. Frostbite can happen in minutes, so there isn't much time to play around with warning signs. Once frostbite begins it's tough to realize how serious the damage is due to lack of feeling, so noticing the color of your skin is telling as to how deep and damaging the frostbite has progressed. Blue and black is the most advanced stage, and damage has likely gone all the way to the bone.

First signs of frostbite:

- Skin has pins and needles feeling.
- Skin turns a pale color.

Later signs:

- Skin hardens and takes on a shiny or waxy appearance.
- Blisters form as skin thaws.

More advanced signs:

- Skin turns a dark blue or black color.
- Skin feels cold to touch and is hard.

Seek medical attention quickly if you or anyone you know is experiencing frostbite, especially at the late and advanced stages. If that's not an option right away, then get to a warm place immediately. Do not rub the affected skin. Soak affected areas in warm (not hot) water or place a warm washcloth over the frostbitten area. As the skin thaws you'll feel a prickly, stinging feeling coming back to your skin. Keep the area covered with loose, dry dressings and place gauze between toes, for example, to keep them separated. Use caution so you don't break any blisters that may have formed.

Frostbite is a bad deal, so do what you can to avoid it:

- Take frequent breaks from the cold.
- Cover your extremities, ears included, with a good hat, gloves, and socks that wick away moisture.
- Wear loose, layered clothing with a first layer of moisture-wicking material.

- Dry off if your clothing becomes wet from sweat or snow as wet clothing makes the likelihood of frostbite higher.

Hypothermia develops when a person's core body temperature falls below ninety-five degrees Fahrenheit, and severe hypothermia develops at a body temperature of eighty-two degrees or lower. Hypothermia is usually caused from extended exposure to cold temperatures, and that risk increases during the cold winter months. When exposed to cold temperatures, our bodies lose heat at a faster rate than it can be produced, so staying out for too long in cold temps uses up our body's storehouse of warmth. This lowering of body temperature is a serious condition, so take steps to avoid it and know how to recognize when it sets in. Note that body temperatures may vary from person to person.

Signs of hypothermia:

- Shivering, which helps the body produce heat with muscle activity
- Weakness, including slow breathing, slow speech, low pulse, drowsiness, and loss of coordination
- Confusion or apathy
- Glassy stare
- For infants, low energy with cold, bright red skin
- Unconsciousness (most serious case)

If you or someone you know is experiencing signs of hypothermia, seek medical attention and call 911, especially if extreme hypothermia has set in, including when body temperature falls below ninety-five degrees Fahrenheit. In the meantime, get to a warmer location and monitor breathing and circulation. Get into dry, warm clothes and begin warming up slowly with blankets and possibly heating pads or electric blankets to core body areas. Keep from warming the body too quickly; warm the core (midsection) first. Try drinking warm liquids, but not alcohol or caffeine.

If the affected person is unconscious, call for medical help right away. If there is no pulse or sign of breathing, immediately begin

CPR (make sure there is no pulse before starting CPR; this may take a bit to know since the heart rate is likely slow). Once CPR is the decided course of action, keep it up until medical help arrives or breathing or a pulse has been restored. Remember that confusion can set in, making the affected person's ability to make good decisions for their safety difficult.

Hypothermia is a scary situation, so take precautions to avoid it:

- Make note of the outside temperature, including wind chill, and don't stay in the cold too long. If necessary, take breaks indoors.
- Dress accordingly by covering exposed skin and dressing in loose, warm layers with water-wicking layers closest to the skin.
- Stay hydrated with warm fluids, excluding alcohol and caffeine, and eat high-fat carbs.
- Stay moving to keep your core warm.
- Take extra precautions with infants, children, elderly, and those who have conditions that increase hypothermia risk (those with diabetes, thyroid conditions, or if using drugs or alcohol).

If you experience any signs of hypothermia, get inside and get warm.

CLOTHING

We get this question a lot: What kinds of clothes should I bring for my visit? Uh, how about all of them?

In northern New Mexico you're going to do this, and it'll be funny when you do: "It's eighty-eight degrees outside with no clouds in the sky. I think I'll leave my jacket. Y'all ready to go?"

Twenty minutes later, somewhere in the mountains: Temperature has dropped into the fifties and the skies are full of cold rain. And you are wet and shivering.

As we discussed earlier, the only thing predictable about weather in the Enchanted Circle is its variability. So you need to bring a variety of clothes to cover the various conditions. In summer, start with a rain jacket, a shell or lightweight jacket, and a fleece jacket or vest. The uniform for veterans includes quick-dry shorts or lightweight pants matched with Tevas/Chacos or sneakers, and to top it off, a fishing shirt (ponytail or man-bun optional). Color choices of clothes match the land and buildings—lots of taupe and ochre and sage. If you are hair-challenged like Mark, bring sunblock and wear a cap.

Evening wear is casual even at fancy eating places. Even if you wear a jacket, no tie is usually needed, and you won't need a fancy jacket or suit coat in any place we know about. One of the great things about the Enchanted Circle is the laid-back aspect of just about everything.

You will see styles of every sort, from turquoise bolo ties and big floppy straw hats to bohemian chic with loose skirts and chiffon tops. Everything goes. But always bring a jacket just in case the weather turns. If you plan to hike, bring a sturdy pair of hiking boots or at least tennis shoes with good grip. We always have sunblock, sunglasses, hat or cap, and a bandana with us. Oh, and bring a pair of swim trunks or your bathing suit in case you get the urge to soak in one of the natural hot springs or a slopeside hot tub.

Winter is tricky. Some years see more snow than others. Some are colder than others. If it's extremely cold outside, wear a shell (waterproof, windproof), a fleece layer, and a warm layer close to your skin. Gloves, scarves, and some sort of warm hat or knit cap on your head are necessary at the ski resorts. On the slopes, skiers wear everything from the most expensive European-style ski suits to Scotch-guarded jeans with a Carhartt jacket. If you plan to drive in the winter, dress warmly and in layers, and bring all your winter gear and drive safely.

DRIVING

To get around the Enchanted Circle, you'll probably be driving. You will at times be seemingly in middle of nowhere, not a car for miles. You might encounter wildlife that jump out in front of your vehicle or appear suddenly as you round a curve—elk herd or bighorn sheep or deer. Keep your eyes on the road and be ready to brake slowly. Make sure your spare tire is aired up and you have a jack that works in case you get a flat tire. What if you end up on a muddy road, or encounter a washed-out side road? Are you prepared? You'll find gas stations in all the main towns, but sometimes you might be 20 miles from the nearest station, so plan accordingly. If you are off-roading, have a spare gas tank (and a fix-it kit). Gas is more expensive in the more remote towns, so expect to pay more.

A common mistake that visitors make, those who aren't used to driving on winding mountain roads, is riding the brake. Don't brake all the way down a curvy mountain road or you may not have any brakes by the time you get down off the mountain. Go into a lower gear and learn to coast through turns. If a vehicle is too close behind you, find a pullout and let them go around you. You need a rest stop or photo op anyway. You might get caught up viewing wildlife or scenery and not realize you are slowing traffic behind you. Stay aware. If you are pulling an RV or trailer camper, stay to the right in two-lane roads, slow down on curves, and be aware of overhanging limbs.

Take your time and enjoy the drive. If you find yourself behind a slow car, there will be a two-lane climbing lane soon enough. Be careful passing if you don't have a line of sight of oncoming traffic. When you approach towns,

Packing List for Your Vehicle or Backpack

- Rain jacket
- Cap or hat
- Sunglasses
- Compass or GPS device
- Fleece jacket
- Bottles or a jug of water
- Breakfast bars, beef jerky, other nonperishables
- Flares and flare gun
- Reflective tape
- Lighter, matches
- Jumper cables
- Tow strap
- Working spare tire and car jack
- Good pocketknife or utility tool

For winter:
- Tire chains for snow
- Kitty litter or something similar for traction
- Folding shovel
- Blanket

communities, parks, and campgrounds, slow down because the speed limit will certainly be lower and you need to watch for kids or dogs. If someone is in the crosswalk waiting to cross, slow down and stop and wait for them to cross.

Many of the backroads only need high clearance, but find out beforehand because you might find yourself in a rutty, muddy situation that requires a 4WD. Especially in fall and winter, roads can ice over or get loaded with dangerous snow pretty quickly, so watch for changing conditions. Things can get hairy suddenly and sometimes authorities will even shut down sections of the road (for instance from Angel Fire to Taos) until they can clear snow and ice. You can find public transportation in several towns too, so you can easily get around or get to and from a ski resort.

GETTING LOST

This is easy to do.

Imagine hiking to a lake and you go off trail for a minute or inadvertently take a side unmarked trail, and you go for a while before you notice that you're not where you're supposed to be. In this big wild country, it's easy to get turned around or lose your bearings.

You can take some precautions to avoid this or to be prepared in case you do get lost. Buy a GPS device. Buy a standard compass. Buy paper maps of the areas you will be traveling and put it in your car or your purse or backpack. These may come in handy if your GPS quits working or runs out of juice. Read the map before you go out driving or hiking.

Look for landmarks before you get lost, and be aware of your surroundings. Know the trails and how they interconnect. Consider if you have a flat tire or if the car breaks down—what then? Are you prepared? Fix up a bag with some survival supplies. What if you slide off an icy road? What if you have to spend the night where you are? Make sure you are prepared for anything that may come up—you won't regret it.

Architecture and Influences of the Region

As you drive through the towns, you will see differences in architecture that emerged from the various historical eras and cultural influences. The Pueblo-style architecture that emerged from Spanish colonial rule is exemplified in the fortified towns with protective walls to hold off against Indian attacks. In these villages, typically some of those along the Rio Grande, you'll see low-slung, flat-roofed adobe houses built around small courtyards called placitas, and narrow streets or lanes.

Taos is the perfect example of this time period. As the Indian threat lessened, the plaza became the center of activity as it attracted people to its annual trade fairs. The French and American fur traders came to the region in the early 1800s and brought Anglo tastes in architecture. Houses built in the Spanish Colonial and Territorial styles stand side by side with Mission and Spanish Pueblo Revival structures. Thick adobe walls made from straw and clay mud kept constant temperatures year-round. Tiny windows held Indian attacks at bay. Houses close together were a Pueblo design, great for efficiency and community.

The Pueblo Indians, prior to invasion, had built condominium-style communities of adobe and stone bricks, with the buildings as high as three or four stories. Their communities were centered on plazas complete with spiritual chambers known as kivas. These Pueblo peoples used the waters of the Rio Grande and its feeder streams to irrigate fields of corn, beans, and squash.

Unique adobe architecture can be seen throughout the Enchanted Circle.

As you walk by the older buildings, you'll see some with round logs protruding from their upper walls. Inside, you can see that these are long round logs, timber rafters, used for structural support. These are called vigas. Warming these adobe buildings are circular adobe fireplaces, usually shallow and built roundly into corners of a room, and also called kivas. These were named after the spiritual centers of Pueblos because of their round shapes.

Vigas inside the Kit Carson House.

Other architectural details that make area homes interesting and distinctive include the colorfully painted doors, window trim, gates, and intricate or colorful tiles everywhere in and out of the house. Adobe needs periodic maintenance, and one thing to note in Taos is that many of the buildings were not originally adobe but have been stuccoed in recent years. The churches are often the best way to see architecture from history, although each one has to have periodic maintenance and construction from time to time.

Hornos are the bee-hived shaped outdoor ovens you will often see in a courtyard (like the Kit Carson House). People can cook many things in these outdoor ovens including bread, but they were used often in summer because it was too hot to fire up an oven inside the house.

Colorful doors adorn the adobe walls.

CAMPING

If you look at a map of the Enchanted Circle, you'll find more campgrounds than you can quickly count, everything from primitive ones off the beaten track to full-fledged hookups, in high desert or alpine, by river or lake, for the tent or big RV, and everything in between. You can camp along numerous rivers including the Rio Grande, Red River, and Rio Costilla. Our favorite might be on the aspen-filled Santa Barbara River. Because of the sudden weather changes, the amazing scenery, proximity to so many outdoor activities, and the varying quality of the campgrounds, camping is always challenging but rewarding in northern New Mexico.

The campgrounds are all over the map in terms of what they offer: some provide clean restrooms, Wi-Fi, water, and electrical hookups, and some offer (at best) a Porta-Potty, if that. You can camp at state parks, national forests, and national monuments, and as crowded as it gets during holidays, it seems there are

There are countless camping opportunities along the Enchanted Circle.

always some campgrounds with room on the Enchanted Circle.

If you camp, put up your food at night, and don't leave out anything that might tempt wild creatures. Use common sense about fires and learn if your campground is under a campfire moratorium. Not all campgrounds have potable water, nor do many have waste water dumps.

WILDLIFE

Don't pet bears. That's for starters. Along the Enchanted Circle, as remote as it is with so little population, the wildlife is plentiful and diverse and interacts often with the towns and their people.

In Red River, it is common to see deer feeding in yards or walking across the street. Bighorn sheep can be found on the roadside east of Questa among other places. If you drive, hike, or spend any time outdoors, you'll see wildlife.

Respect the wildlife. Don't feed the animals. Respect distance with any animal, not only for your safety but for theirs. You might see eagles, marmots, bighorn sheep, deer, and elk all in one day. Marmots are known as whistling pigs, the fat furry critters that crawl around the rocky slopes. In the lower elevations, you might see snakes—in particular, rattlesnakes. Just watch where you put your hands and keep an eye out as you hike or climb.

We see lots of birders around the Enchanted Circle. The Enchanted Circle is great for birding, or so we're told and so we read, but we aren't birders. We see birds and know Western Tanagers, red-tailed hawks, golden eagles, hummingbirds, magpies, Canada jays, chickadees, and woodpeckers, but other than that . . . we just don't know our birds.

Wildlife You Might See around the Enchanted Circle

- Marmot
- Bighorn sheep
- Mule deer
- Elk
- Rattlesnake
- Peregrine falcon
- Black bear
- Tarantula
- River otter
- Red-tailed hawk

- Bald eagle
- Golden eagle
- Hummingbird
- Albert squirrel
- Wild turkey
- Prairie dog
- Pika
- Mountain lion (you almost never see one, but they're around)

And the list goes on and on. Have fun putting together your own list of all the wildlife you see on your trip.

Beware of Bears

Bears live in the Enchanted Circle. You probably won't see one. You might see one from a distance while you are hiking. You possibly could see one cross the road. The only sure way to see a bear is to foolishly leave food outside overnight.

Bears are intelligent creatures and have an amazing sense of smell. It doesn't take long for a bear to realize that improperly stored garbage is an easy source of food. The pattern of events is predictable: A bear feeds on garbage and people enjoy the spectacle. After a few visits, the bear loses its fear of humans because the lure of garbage is greater than its natural tendency to avoid people. When the bear no longer fears humans, someone usually gets hurt and the bear is put down.

The best approach to avoid all this is to "bear-proof" your property by storing food, garbage, and other attractants (dog food and bones and treats, or an uncleaned barbecue grill, for example) away from bears. To decrease odors, store garbage in tightly tied or heavy-duty bags in bear-resistant dumpsters or garbage cans. You'll find these receptacles in most of the towns along the Enchanted Circle. If a bear-proof container is not available, store the garbage indoors until it can be taken to a refuse site. Take advantage of regular trash pickup services.

By the way, black bears come in a variety of colors, including cinnamon, honey, blonde, and reddish. You won't find any grizzly bears since they last walked in New Mexico over one hundred years ago.

Black bear exploring near Taos Ski Valley.

FISHING
in the Enchanted Circle

The Enchanted Circle offers some of the best trout fishing in the state and in the Southwest. You could fish for pike in a high-desert river in the morning and rare cutthroat trout in a pristine creek in the afternoon. You can fish in rivers and creeks in so many climates and in high desert streams, alpine brooks, small wild creeks, high country lake, tailwaters, and spring-fed year-round rivers. The trout waters of the Enchanted Circle offer fishing for all four seasons, private and public, beginner and advanced, and you can find lots of fly-fishing shops and tackle stores, rentals, guides, and outfitters. The kicker is the gorgeous native Rio Grande cutthroat you can catch, an ancient fish that only inhabits 7 percent of its original habitat and is found in several regional streams.

For fly fishers, the area has some notable hatches including a not-to-miss caddis hatch on the Rio Grande in late May. You will see stoneflies early, and caddis and mayfly throughout the rest of summer and fall. Grasshoppers make their presence known in August. Make sure to drop into a fly shop or two and pick up some local patterns that work better than your generic patterns. They can also clue you in to some techniques that work well in different waters.

The Rio Grande will demand at the least a 4-weight outfit, but we recommend a 5 or 6 weight. The other streams are small to medium, so if you fish a 3 or 4 weight, you'll be fine. Sometimes the wind will kick up on some streams, especially the Rio Costilla, and that requires a heavier rod. For bait and spin fishers, the Rio Grande is ideal for your hardware and bait. You will want to make sure that you are fishing in water that allows your lure or bait because many waters have sections that are fly fishing only.

As far as keeping fish, you don't want to keep any more than is allowed by regulation; and if you have to keep fish, keep stocked fish over wild. Be careful walking through redds (trout egg laying areas), and take care in releasing fish.

Because of the patchwork of federal and state administration of these rivers, regulations vary from stretch to stretch. Buy an appropriate license. Although you have hundreds of miles of public water, if you want something different, hook up with a guide or fly shop to get into private water. Each town has at least one fly shop and several guides, and they can offer half-day and full-day trips and even float trips.

You might wonder whether you'll need to wear chest waders. That's a personal choice, but in summer, wet wading or just hip waders are often all you'll need. In the Rio Grande all year, and in other fisheries in fall and winter, the water gets cold, so we say yes to chest waders. Many fly shops rent rods and waders.

The great fishing of this trip begins at Taos then moves north to Questa, east to Red River, and settles southward to Eagle Nest. In a week's time, you could fish the huge canyon waters of the Rio Grande for gargantuan pike and large browns, and then wade the intimate waters of the Cimarron River for wild brown trout that rise willingly to dry flies. You could angle in the rocky pools of the consistent Rio Hondo and then hike into the lower Red River to nymph for migrating cuttbows. You'll enjoy a variety of fisheries, a diversity of fish, waters good for spin, bait, and fly anglers, and waters that

The Rio Pueblo is an underrated trout fishery.

range from meadow streams to canyon rivers, to big water, to intimate water and a big mountain reservoir. You could also boat around the big mountain reservoir, Eagle Nest Lake, fishing for cutts, snagging kokanee salmon and enjoying the mountain vistas of Wheeler Peak and Mount Baldy. Here's a breakdown of fishing in the Enchanted Circle:

RIO PUEBLO

This is the great-looking pocket stream that flows along the NM 518, from Tres Ritos, past Sipapu, past the Taos turnoff where it then follows NM 75 all the way to where it meets up with Rio Santa Barbara and forms Rio Embudo. From there, it dumps into the Rio Grande.

So how does it fish? We like it and fish it a lot, finding it has mostly stocked rainbows and some brown trout. The river sees lots of anglers (it's by the road after all) but mostly at the easy access points. So here's how to get to the pools and runs and pocket water: get in the water and wade away from the access points. You'll find numerous pullouts and access points along the river. The trout aren't big and they aren't often wild, but the river is only twenty minutes from Taos and you can find entire stretches all to yourself. The river is good for fly or spin fishing. La Junta feeds Rio Pueblo and is fun for dapping for smaller trout.

The river gets a good amount of traffic at the easy access points and large pools, but for the most part Rio Pueblo is an ideal getaway spot for anglers. No, it's not of the quality of the lower Red River, doesn't have the trout density of Cimarron River, or provide the beauty of Rio Santa Barbara, but the rocky roadside river provides 15 to 20 miles of fishable, accessible trout-laden opportunity only twenty minutes south of Taos.

You'll catch a mixture of wild and stocked trout, browns and rainbows. From its confluence with Santa Barbara to form Rio Embudo to its upper reaches at La Junta, anglers have pocket water, loaded with in-stream rocks and boulders, overhanging brush and limbs, trees, deep pools and shallow runs, and opportunities to fish all by yourself.

RIO SANTA BARBARA

This high-mountain cold clear stream is one of the unsung gems in the northern part of the state. You probably won't find better cutthroat fishing than here. It's likely the best backpacking public river in the region. Anglers have three forks to choose from and each has its own personality. Oh, and it's also the most beautiful river and has the most pristine scenery of all the fishable rivers in northern New Mexico. You'll be fishing in high altitude (9,000–12,000 feet).

While known for its colorful wild cutthroats, we've been catching more and more good-sized brown trout. This is unfortunate because it means that the native cutthroat that used to swim in the upper stream waters are being crowded out. The higher you go, the more cutts you'll catch.

To get there from Taos, take NM 518 south to NM 75 and turn right (west). It'll run into NM 73 which you'll turn left on. Watch closely from here—a little over a mile you'll see FR 116. Stay left and follow the sign leading to Santa Barbara Campground. Here's your home base for a great afternoon or a few days. You can fish the river along the road near the campground and downstream for 3 miles.

Most anglers hike up and fish the West Fork (aka upper Santa Barbara). It's the largest of the forks and has the best developed trail, a pleasant hike, and lots of different trout water habitat. There is a stream crossing over a log that can be interesting. You can also hike up the Middle Fork or East Fork if you don't mind being all by yourself in beautiful, wild, mountainous country.

RIO EMBUDO

Formed by the confluence of Rio Santa Barbara and Rio Pueblo, this is a decent, but very pretty, brown trout stream that fishes best in cool spring and fall and runs west along NM 75.

EMBUDO BOX

This little tributary of the Rio Grande is one of the prettiest places on the planet, and the fishing's not bad either. Embudo means "funnel" in Spanish, and this place lives up to its name. The river foams through a deep gorge of layered sandstone. There are no real trails down; anglers must scramble. A 4WD to get there is a must. Once at the water, your reward is feisty little browns. The window to fish the Embudo is short, and spring is your best bet. Flows between 35 and 80 CFS are fishiest.

RIO CHIQUITO, POT CREEK, LITTLE RIO GRANDE

These are small streams south of Taos, ideal for dry fly fishing. You'll find little wild trout, lots of brush, and good camping spots. Access the streams from NM 518 south from Taos. NM 518

Angler fishing the Rio Chiquito.

follows Little Rio Grande; FR 437 runs alongside miles and miles of Rio Chiquito; and FR 438 follows Pot Creek (also known as Rito de la Olla).

RIO PUEBLO DE TAOS

This is almost exclusively a cold-weather fishery because the water heats up and the rocks and boulders get slippery. The only public water is on the last few miles of the river before it dumps into the Rio Grande near Taos Junction Bridge. It can be tough wading at times because of the slippery rocks, but the pocket water holds some big trout, both browns and rainbows. Rio Pueblo de Taos fishes well in fall and even in the snowy days of winter.

CABRESTO CREEK AND LAKE

This alpine lake is loaded with cutthroat and brook trout, but getting there is not all that easy. Passenger vehicles can make it if there is no rain, but to be safe we recommend a high-clearance vehicle, preferably a 4WD. Take NM 38 north through Questa, turn north at NM 563/FR 134. Follow the gravel road to the turnoff at FR 134A. Follow this for a short ways till you reach the lake. The lake is hard to fish from the bank (weedy) so you'll want to consider a float tube. The 12 miles of bubbly creek are productive but brushy and small, loaded with small brook, brown, rainbow, and cutthroat trout. FR 134 runs alongside the creek.

RIO GRANDE

This is a big river with miles and miles of rugged angling and plenty of access points. The Rio Grande is one of the wildest, one of the most productive, and one of the most unsung fisheries in the West. Fish by wading, standing on the bank, or by floating a raft.

This big river used to enjoy a reputation in the 1950s and 1960s as one of the top trout spots in the nation, but the river's trout population and the numbers of large fish declined in the 1970s and 1980s. Today, to a large degree, the river has recovered.

The Rio Grande cuts a mighty path on its 70-mile southward course from Colorado, through the wide valleys and a deep rift. The Rio Grande is a wide freestone river with deep pools, wide glides, boulders, big pocket water, and riffles, and is inaccessible except in a few places due to the 600- to 1,000-foot deep canyon. Various springs and several streams feed the river.

Pike have become the winter draw on the river. Look for deep, slow pools and fish rainbow trout streamers and hold on. Trout lovers can drop a line for big browns and fat rainbows and a decent population of cutthroat trout. Cast around rocks, along current edges, foam eddies, and at the head and tail of pools.

For trout, use an 8.5- to 9-foot rod for 5- or 6-weight lines. Anglers will want an 8- or 9-weight outfit for pike. Pack a daypack, first aid kit, and some warm clothes. You won't need to wade, so wear hiking boots with good ankle support. Allow plenty of time to get into the canyon and start hiking out early. This is not for the faint of heart because there are some very steep trails.

Runoff in late May can be heavy, but the Rio Grande is productive year-round. You're in for a serious hike along rugged trails to reach many of the best and out-of-the-way spots. There are a number of trails leading to the river. Most are steep, many are unmarked, and many shouldn't be tried unless you are in good shape. It's a long way down and a long way back out.

If the water is off color and high, fish to the edges and in clearer water.

No need to fish when the sun is off the water. Fish late and leave early. For light hiking, the best access to the Rio Grande is at the John Dunn Bridge, west of Arroyo Hondo, at the confluence of the Rio Hondo and Rio Grande. As you travel north on NM 522, you will cross the bridge over Rio Hondo and turn left (west) on B006 and, after a bit, B007 to go to John Dunn Bridge over Rio Grande. The river can also be reached at Pilar, at the confluence of the Red River and in several points in the Wild and Scenic River National Recreation Area.

COYOTE CREEK

This is a highly fished, highly stocked small stream south of Angel Fire. From Angel Fire, take NM 434 south about 30 miles. You'll enjoy a twisting, narrow road to get there, but you'll also enjoy a half day angling for small wild browns and stocked rainbow trout in a pretty place.

You can fish in Coyote Creek State Park, a pretty little park in a valley famous for its wildflowers and forests of pine and spruce. Lots of sections of the creek have riparian habitat, willows and cottonwood trees, that will interrupt your casts, but there are some nice open meadow stretches too. There are several miles of public fishing outside of the park but the trout are skittish so be invisible.

Don't wear the chest waders; this is small, shallow water ideal for wet wading and fly fishing. The public water is limited but marked. Because of the tightness and difficulty, the stream doesn't get lots of pressure. The

creek is less than 10 feet across in most places and has lots of brush and overhanging limbs to mess with your casting. The two access points are Coyote Creek State Park and Harold Brock Fishing Area.

CIMARRON RIVER

The Cimarron River shouldn't be overlooked. A twenty-nine-

Angler fishing the confluence of the Rio Grande and Red River.

inch, nine-pound brown trout was caught in its quality water section a couple of years ago. This dry-fly haven has some of the highest density of catchable trout in the southwest.

From Eagle Nest, take US 64 east through scenic low-slung mountains that spill into the fishing town of Eagle Nest. Eagle Nest Lake is loaded with rainbow trout, mackinaw, and kokanee salmon. The Cimarron flows from Eagle Nest Lake, so the tandem is close enough that you can fish and enjoy both in a single day. You can park at any number of pullouts in the 8-mile stretch. There may be a car at every pullout, but don't be discouraged. Find a parking spot and just hike a bit. Soon you'll have plenty of water to yourself. We recommend a guide for your first go at the Cimarron. It's a tailwater, and while the choppiness and freestone nature will have you believing it fishes with big dry flies, you're going to have a long day until you figure out the hatches, the feeding times, and the locations where the wild browns and stocked rainbows tend to hang throughout the day.

Spin fishermen will have success when the water is up, but when the flows are low, you'll be in for a long day casting Rooster Tails and Panther Martins through skinny pools.

Cimarron trout enjoy bounteous and regular hatches, so fly anglers have a definite advantage. Remember to respect distance from other anglers in this tight river. The chances are good you will lose a few flies in the branches and willows. Over the years we've seen many black bears walking along the river and the road, so you'll need to keep your head on a swivel and give them room and have a great day fishing.

The Cimarron River has a high density of wild brown trout.

WI-FI AND CELLULAR SERVICE

The cellular service is surprisingly good throughout the Enchanted Circle. Many hotels and lodges and cabins as well as coffeehouses and restaurants offer free Wi-Fi, so you should be able to catch up on news and emails. You may use up a lot of data when you drive out of Wi-Fi range, so you may want to put your phone on airplane mode until you can get service again.

RECREATIONAL ACTIVITIES

MOUNTAIN BIKING AND ROAD CYCLING

The Enchanted Circle is one of the mountain biking meccas of the Southwest, including Angel Fire, Taos Ski Valley, Red River, and too numerous forest roads and trails to name. You will find a number of bike shops that can provide info, gear, lessons, advice, and guides.

The road riding of the area is as underrated as it is challenging. The rides offer epic scenery and world-class climbing, but the roads are not entirely bike friendly—often rough and narrow with little or no shoulder. Since the roads are rough, be prepared by bringing spare tubes and a patch kit. Bring enough water because the summer days can get hotter than you think.

The Enchanted Circle offers rides that range from short, town loops to several century options. You can get more info from several bike shops. As anywhere, crime can happen, so be on the safe side and bring a lock.

The Angel Fire Resort's trails are a biker's paradise. (Photo credit: Michael Fiore, Outdoor Element Sports.)

OFF-ROADING 4WD/ATV/OHV

Visitors enjoy a lot of options for off-roading and jeeping around the Enchanted Circle, but Red River, Angel Fire, and Questa are the heavily favored spots. Plenty of businesses rent jeeps and OHVs but you can also hire guides.

Red River is an ideal place to go four-wheel exploring because of all the old mining roads and forest service roads in any direction from town. This area has so much public land that you have hundreds of miles of trails. Escorted tours are available, or if you prefer you can go it alone along a series of well-marked area trails. Explore old mining camps and drive along canyon rivers through alpine environments. Take care not to hurt the land because at this altitude, scars on the land take years, sometimes centuries, to heal. So stay on the marked trails, minimize wheel spin, don't gouge the trail, and avoid mud when possible to avoid rutting. Cross streams only at designated fording points where the trail crosses the stream.

Go alone or hire local tour operators. Guided tours are an ideal way for families to safely learn the history, natural history, ghost stories, and other lore on their trip. Trips to abandoned cabins and gold mines—and gold panning—are often part of the experience.

HIKING AND BACKPACKING

If you want to hike into history, backpack into wilderness, or trek through some of the most breathtaking scenery you've ever seen, then you're in the right area. From the Bureau of Land Management sites to national monuments, state parks to national forests, you can find everything from an easy hour-long hike to a multi-day backpacking trek.

Because you are hiking in wild country, you must be prepared for any number of contingencies: snakes, mountain lions, bears, sudden and inclement weather, getting lost, sprained ankles, heat exhaustion, dehydration, and trail closures. Get the appropriate maps—yes, real paper maps—and look them over, study them. Put them in your pocket in case your GPS doesn't work. Check with experts or shops before you go to learn about up-to-date conditions. Know before you go.

Backpackers and their four-legged pal traverse the trail toward Williams Lake.

Be prepared and don't hike alone. Imagine the worst and prepare.

On longer or more difficult hikes, pack some extra food and water, and bring a way to purify water. One of the biggest dangers of the Enchanted Circle hikes is dehydration, especially at lower elevations where it can get much hotter than you ever thought. Although the rivers and springs look clean, they are not clean enough for drinking. You do not want to catch "beaver fever" or Giardiasis, an intestinal illness caused by a microscopic parasite called Giardia lamblia. You can be laid up for days with diarrhea and fever.

Changes in weather can happen rapidly, so while you may see a clear blue sky and think, "I can leave behind my rain jacket or fleece," you do so at your own peril. Put a jacket in your light backpack or wrap one around your waist. You're gonna need it.

At lower elevations, encountering snakes—specifically, rattlesnakes—is always a possibility. When you grab a rock to pull yourself up, be aware that in that hole a rattler might live.

Walking sticks or poles are not always necessary but help to maintain balance in uneven and loose footing. Although Enchanted Circle trails, lower and higher elevations alike, are well maintained, there are enough holes and loose rocks that if you aren't cognizant, an accident can happen suddenly and ruin your hike. So no matter what hike, take plenty of water, snacks, a small first aid kit, and buddies, and alert others when and where you go. Sign in if there is a sign-in sheet. If you backpack, make sure you learn about where you can camp and where you can start a fire.

HOT AIR BALLOONING

The air balloon outfitters will soar high in the blue sky and drop into or over the gorge, over the mesa, and above the mountains. They offer sunrise balloon trips, champagne balloon trips, or customized trips. They have a great safety record. You can bring a camera or video cam and see things from a new perspective, looking down on the world to see exquisite panoramas of the Taos Valley.

A horseback riding group makes its way back to the stables after a trail ride near Angel Fire.

HORSEBACK RIDING

Numerous outfitters and ranches offer various horseback riding excursions ranging from a one-hour ride to backcountry overnight trips.

LLAMA TREKKING

Several outfitters will pack llamas with gear and hike you into the pristine wilderness. You can just go for a day picnic or camp overnight or for a few days. Llamas are sweet, gentle, fun animals that will help provide unique family fun for single-day and multi-day adventures. They're a great way to enjoy ecotourism. Guides will teach you about flora and fauna, history, and geography.

WINTER SPORTS

Types of winter sports include downhill skiing, snowboarding, UTV snowcat skiing, sleighing, sledding, ice skating, and ice fishing. Choose from Taos Ski Resort, Angel Fire Ski Resort, Red River Ski Resort, Sipapu Ski Resort, and Enchanted Forest, and then you've got snowshoeing, cross-country skiing, snowmobiling, back-basin skiing, and more. It's a winter wonderland. At each ski resort, you can enjoy great après-ski, live music, restaurants, cafés, and bars. If you go into the backcountry, take the time to learn about avalanche safety.

Taos Ski Valley offers all types of wintertime sports.

CUISINE
of Northern New Mexico

One of the major draws to the Enchanted Circle is the food. The cuisine of northern New Mexico has an international flavor, a beautiful exchange of ingredients and recipes and elements from so many cultures. Influenced by history, New Mexican cuisine is an interesting mix of Pueblo Indian, Spanish, Mexican, Anglo, cowboy chuckwagon, and even French and Mediterranean. The cuisine reflects what each culture brought to the region and also what the region could grow or raise. Each culture contributed elements of their own to the indigenous menu (corn, chile, beans, squash, etc.).

The Spaniards notably brought their cuisine to the region including rice, wheat, lamb, and especially beef. The Indians taught the Spanish conquerors about corn and all the ways to prepare it (roasted, pudding, stewed, cornbread, cornmeal, posole, etc.) as well as introducing them to chile peppers, a crop indigenous to the New World. The climate and palates of the peoples determined what grew, what didn't, what they liked to eat, what they did not. Perhaps only New Orleans has seen such a food fusion of cultures while embracing culinary traditions. So the region has had wave after wave of newcomers who have introduced their culinary elements to the existing gastronomy.

The staple ingredients in New

Freshly roasted green chilis are delicious and should not be missed.

Cheese-stuffed, battered, and fried chili rellenos.

Mexican cuisine include chiles, corn, and beans; these are all grown locally. Other common ingredients include cheese, tortillas, onions, beef, chicken, and pork. Some tools any northern New Mexican cook might use include a mortar and pestle (small bowl that is used to grind ingredients like garlic, chiles, seeds, pepper, cloves, fresh herbs, and avocado), a micaceous clay pot (to cook and serve soups, beans, etc.) and a comal (to make and warm tortillas). You might see that rice, a staple of Tex-Mex, is not often on the menu in restaurants; that's because corn (or hominy) is the starch of choice.

Did you know that chile and frijoles are the official state vegetables of New Mexico? Green chile cheeseburgers are a common and basic Northern New Mexican staple comfort food. It's as simple as topping a burger with roasted, chopped New Mexican green chile and cheese. You can get this burger at any burger joint and most restaurants.

Don't come to northern New Mexico and eat at the same fast food place you have in your home city. Try something new, something local, something you haven't tried before. The food can be hot to taste from different peppers or chiles or ingredients because such is the nature of food from this state, so check on your menu if there is a hot warning or ask your server. Treat yourself with a sopaipilla with honey and butter. Sopaipillas are so amazing; you can eat a stuffed one with meat and chile on it for your meal too. Oh, the region has great and underrated wines, so make sure to try a bottle or two.

Discover the Regional Food

You're a newbie to New Mexican food and get seated in a restaurant. Now what? If you are not familiar with New Mexican food, the menu may be confusing. Here are some explanations of the terms you are reading:

Biscochitos or Bizcochitos: A crispy butter cookie flavored with cinnamon and anise that is the state cookie of New Mexico. Served every December, it's a holiday tradition for northern New Mexico. The dough is rolled and traditionally cut into the shape of stars and crescent moons.

Buñuelos: Deep-fried fritter popular around Christmas and New Year's Day.

Calabacitas: Sautéed dish consisting of squash, zucchini, onions, and sometimes other items like chile or corn.

Carne Adovada: Usually this tasty dish is long-simmered pork chunks in a red chile stew.

Carne Asada: Marinated beef, grilled and sliced thin.

Carnitas: Braised, simmered, or roasted pork, usually shredded and served in little pieces (which is what carnitas means).

Chile Relleno: Usually mild chile pepper stuffed with cheese, meat, or both; served fried or naked.

Chimichanga: Deep-fried burrito usually covered in chile.

Chorizo: Spicy pork sausage heavily flavored with red chile, garlic, peppers, and other ingredients.

Flan: Sweetened egg custard dessert with a caramel topping.

Green Chile Stew: A stew made with green chiles and potatoes. Usually served with chopped or shredded pork in it and often topped with sour cream.

Green chili stew with pork.

Ordering Christmas to taste both red and green chili.

Green or red? You'll hear locals respond to that question with "Christmas," meaning they'll take both red and green chile on their food. Each restaurant café makes its chile differently, so when you ask which is hotter, well, it just depends. You can always ask for it on the side to decide for yourself. What a local might think is mild just might make you cough and burn your throat.

Guacamole/Avocado: Great for chip dipping, avocado is a buttery, light-green, oily-flesh fruit that is obviously sent from the gods. Have them make you tableside guacamole, a dip made from avocados. We take avocados as part of our backpacking trips or streamside picnics, a snack good all by itself.

Helado Frito: Fried ice cream. We know, right—how can you fry ice cream? Don't worry about how, just order it and enjoy the unique texture and rich flavors.

Huevos Rancheros: Hearty breakfast of fried or poached eggs on top of stacked tortillas or a fried corn tortilla with a sauce, usually served with refried beans.

Indian Fry Bread: Thin, fried dough paired with either savory (beans, lettuce, meat) or sweet (honey or powdered sugar) tastes.

Michelada: There are numerous variations on this drink, but it's basically a cold beer prepared with lime juice, tomato juice, hot sauces, spices, and peppers served in a salt-rimmed chilled glass.

Migas: Pronounced MEE-gus or MEE-guz, migas recipes vary but the most common is a combination of scrambled eggs with tomatoes, peppers, onions, cheese, and crumbled corn tortilla strips.

Migas, a hearty New Mexican breakfast.

Pico de Gallo: A chilled adornment to your meal made from chopped tomato, onion, cilantro, pepper (usually serrano but also jalapeño), salt, lime juice, and sometimes other ingredients. The words translate to "beak of the rooster."

Piñon coffee: Coffee flavored with piñon. Try it. The taste is amazing, smooth, and nutty. By the way, coffeehouse culture is alive and well here in northern New Mexico, so if you need to get your espresso fix or order a decaf soy latte with an extra shot and cream, or some other fancy coffee drink, they've got you covered.

Poblano: A mild, dark green pepper, used in recipes or served stuffed with cheese or meat.

Posole: Thick soup or stew with pork (sometimes chicken, sometimes no meat) and hominy, garlic, and chile. Great for cold days. Often served as a side.

Tamales: Usually served with a main dish but can be its own main meal. Steamed masa dough rolled with meat (pork or ground meat or sometimes beans) and crushed peppers, wrapped in cornhusks.

Tres Leches: Also called pan tres leches, meaning "three milks bread." This is a sponge cake soaked and flavored in evaporated milk, condensed milk, and heavy cream.

Award-winning wines offered along the Enchanted Circle.

Wine: New Mexico has a long winemaking history dating back to the seventeenth century when monks smuggled in vines for making sacramental wines. Spaniards who settled the area also brought their winemaking skills and grapevine-growing techniques to the Southwest. Italians had their hand in starting New Mexico wines too when the Jesuit monks brought their own techniques and varietals. This part of New Mexico has a great little collection of quality wineries and tasting rooms. Visit with vintners, sample wines, and take some home as souvenirs. Local wineries can be found on the New Mexico True Wine Trail, so check with the Taos Visitor Center for maps and specifics.

New Mexican Sights Commonly Found

Drums: Rawhide drums are a traditional instrument of Native American tribes and a staple in their music. Traditional drums are handmade out of hollowed-out logs, usually aspen, pine, or cottonwood, and stitched with rawhide on either end. Rhythmic drumbeats were played in times of celebration, ceremonial dances, or before going into battle. Purchase hand-fashioned examples at the Taos Pueblo.

Kiva: New Mexican-style beehive fireplace. Originally, kiva referred to a round underground meeting place used for religious rituals by male Pueblo Indians of the Southwest.

A handmade drum at the Taos Pueblo makes an unforgettable gift.

Moccasins: Shoes typically made of deerskin or another soft, tanned leather, sole included. Moccasin styles vary; some are adorned with beads or embroidery. Moccasins were historically worn by many North American Indian tribes, hunters, trappers, and traders.

Piñon nuts or pinyon nuts: These are the edible seeds of the piñon trees, a great nutty snack. You'll often see these in New Mexican cuisine and adorning food. You can also find piñon-flavored local coffee. Piñon wood is most often used in New Mexico kivas and fireplaces and it has a unique fragrant aroma. Piñon nuts are often sold from roadside trucks and at local markets.

Pottery: Much of the traditional Indian pottery found here is made from clay of the Sangre de Cristo Mountains and is known as micaceous pottery. It is particularly unique due to the sparkling flecks of mica found in the soil, giving the pieces their golden sheen. These shiny specks may be why the Spanish conquistadors thought this area was one of the Seven Cities of

Cibola, or cities of gold. Lots of potters, besides the Native Americans, can be found in New Mexico creating beautiful, unique pieces of art.

Retablo: A Mexican folk art, devotional painting depicting a physical representation of holy images, often of a saint, Christ, or the Virgin Mother. Brought to the area by Franciscan monks, they were later removed by Bishop Lamy after the conquest by the US Army. Luckily the formation of the Spanish Colonial Arts Society in 1924 helped bring this artistic tradition back to New Mexico. Retablos are often painted on wood and made of natural materials.

Colorful ristras decorate storefronts, walkways, and doorways.

Ristras: It's a rope of dried chiles strung together, usually red, but these can also be made with dried garlic or corn. You'll see these hanging all over New Mexico in front of houses, in kitchens, everywhere, and they're commonly found at farmers' markets. They were originally a way for old-timey food storage, but they're typically for decoration today. Some come in wreath or heart shapes. Some say this traditional New Mexican decoration brings good luck and health.

Turquoise jewelry: Turquoise is a common gem found in New Mexico and the Southwest, as it forms in these arid climates. Turquoise has been collected and used by Native American tribes for thousands of years for trade, adornment, jewelry, and art. This Southwestern stone became more commonly used in the jewelry we think of as Indian turquoise jewelry once the Spanish brought over their craft of silverwork and the Native Americans combined it with stonecutting skills of their own. Turquoise ranges in shades of blue to green depending on the metals in the soil where it formed. The bluer the turquoise, the more copper; the greener the turquoise, the more iron. Turquoise jewelry has become iconically identified with the Southwest and you can find many hand-tooled pieces here.

HIGH ROAD TO TAOS

The High Road to Taos is a designated scenic byway from Santa Fe to Taos, traveling north from US 84/285 and following along NM 503. It can take two to four hours or more to travel, depending on how you decide to traverse this piece of land—driving straight through or stopping for photo opportunities, gallery visits, and historic sites. No matter your choice, try to immerse yourself in the beauty of the varied and unique landscape as you drive. Reflect on the ancient people who lived here so long ago, and keep in mind those who bravely began these little Spanish villages along the route.

Travel this 67-mile-long road through old Hispanic villages full of art and history. This stretch of New Mexico is known mostly for its incredible art influence and being an artists' haven. In fact, every year in September there is the High Road Art Tour (see page 67) to showcase some of the artists around Taos. The scenery of the High Road is a notable bonus that you can't miss either, with gorgeous peaks and hillsides, meadows and canyons, orchards and foliage, desert and forests. Each season brings about a different color palette to the landscape worth soaking in and photographing. Remember, it's not always about the destination but also about the journey and how you get there.

Left to right, top: entrance gate to San José de Gracia Church; marker signifying the Jack M. Campbell Highway traversing the beautiful Southwest landscape. Bottom: place of worship in Chimayó; welcome sign to El Santuario de Chimayó.

JOURNEY TO
EL SANTUARIO DE CHIMAYÓ

15 Santuario Drive, Chimayó, NM 87522

(505) 351-9961

From Santa Fe, take US 84/285 north, go east on NM 503 to County Road 98. You'll drive into a valley and in a short time come to the second stop along this winding route. Off to the right, you'll see the turnoff and a sign to El Santuario de Chimayó's parking.

Chimayó is a special little village and the most famous stop along the High Road to Taos. It started out as a Spanish farming settlement in the seventeenth century where the ancient Tewa pueblo once stood. Later into the eighteenth century, the plaza and surrounds were designed to resist Indian attack, and today the village feels like stepping into another place and time. The shops in Chimayó carry lots of religious art and retablos plus bags of cultural spices, including the area's rich, red chile powder. The well-known Chimayó families,

The famous El Santuario de Chimayó along the High Road to Taos.

Ortega and Trujillo, produce artistic, traditional weavings, which can be found in the Chimayó stores. You'll also find local art and souvenirs tucked away in the village shops.

The town of Chimayó is famous for El Santuario de Chimayó and the famed el pocito where hopefuls can gather a bit of sacred soil to cure their ills. The sanctuary was designated as a National Historic Landmark in 1970. The smaller side chapel, or prayer room, is famous for its holy dirt and stories of healings. Crutches, photos, walkers, and shrines line the walls of this unique chapel and fill it with prayers and thankfulness for healing. Enter a small door at the end of the prayer room to el pocito to find the blessed earth, known for its curative powers. Bring a baggie or a vial of some sort to carry home a few ounces of Chimayó's curative soil for yourself, even if you don't need it now. Amazingly, twenty-five to thirty tons of soil are taken from el pocito each year, so the church must bless and replenish the famed soil.

The church itself makes no claim of the soil's curative powers, but many stories corroborate the historic tales. Either way, many come in faith and prayer, many come to take a chance, and many for curiosity.

One legend of this blessed soil's beginnings began in the early 1800s. A local friar was giving penances and noticed a beam of light emanating from the hillside, where he unearthed a crucifix. One of the area's priests took the crucifix to Santa Cruz chapel, but three different times it disappeared and miraculously returned to its original spot in the soil. It was deemed that this was where it should remain, and hence the building of the famed chapel and stories of healing began. The current adobe chapel is the second and larger chapel built on this sacred ground. The crucifix found on this site is still present in the main chapel.

Thousands come here during Holy Week, the week before Easter, as part of a religious pilgrimage. Known as "Lourdes of the Southwest," this pilgrimage is considered the most significant Catholic pilgrimage in the United States. Many of the pilgrims make the 7-mile walk from Española, but many trek from Santa Fe and as far away as Albuquerque and beyond. It is quite a sight to see the procession of pilgrims walking day and night, some carrying crosses, some crawling, and some walking with thorns piercing their feet. Some are making the journey for thanksgiving, some for grace and enlightenment, and some for intercession.

Santo Niño de Atocha, Children's Chapel

6 Santuario Drive, Chimayó, NM 87522

(505) 351-9961

Make sure to visit the nearby Santo Niño de Atocha at this stop. The traditional story that led to this chapel in Chimayó dates back hundreds and hundreds of years to the Christ Child, or Santo Niño, who would wander about on missions of help. In the mid-1800s, a Chimayó local from an influential family, Serveriano Medina, became extremely ill. Upon his recovery he journeyed to Mexico to the shrine of Santo Niño de Atocha to pay homage and give thanks for his blessings of recovery. Santo Niño had been known for many miracles in Spain and Mexico for years. Medina returned to Chimayó with a papier-mâché creation of Santo Niño and built a chapel in 1856 to house the Christ Child doll, bringing Santo Niño even more devotees. Today, the chapel is considered a children's chapel, but visitors still leave gifts in the prayer room—most commonly children's shoes. The shoes are often given to Santo Niño so that this caregiving child will

always have a clean pair of shoes to wear when on the next mission of help, but many leave the shoes with notes for intercession or thankfulness. Interestingly, the original papier-mâché doll brought back from Plateros in Zacatecas, Mexico, in the mid-1800s still resides in the chapel.

VISIT THE
SAN JOSÉ DE GRACIA CHURCH

2

2377-2381 NM 76, Chamisal, NM 87521

(505) 351-4360

From Chimayó, travel north on NM 76 passing
through Truchas to Trampas.

Las Trampas began in 1751 with the Spanish land grant Santo Tomas Apostol del Rio de las Trampas. Trampas, meaning "traps," was so named for the beaver traps set by settlers. The historic church here, San José de Gracia, is a National Historic Landmark with traditional adobe architecture and topped with wooden steeples. The rugged mission, finished in 1776, sits in the center of town and is easy to see. When leaving Las Trampas, look off to the right to see an old Spanish aqueduct made with a wooden flume that still transports water into town for agricultural purposes.

The Las Trampas Land Grant is also home to the village of Chamisal just ahead on NM 76. Most believe that the name, Chamisal,

Ruggedly beautiful, the historic mission church welcomes visitors.

is from the Chrysothamnus bush, often called a Chamisa shrub, which turns a beautiful golden hue as fall approaches. When the sun starts to get lower on the horizon, the colors here glow no matter the season.

3 STEP INTO HISTORY AT SAN FRANCISCO DE ASÍS

60 St. Francis Plaza, Ranchos de Taos, NM 87557
(575) 758-2754
From Trampas, continue north on NM 76 past Peñasco and past Vadito. Turn north on NM 518 and go on into Taos.

A must-visit on the Enchanted Circle, this iconic parish in Ranchos de Taos (4 miles south of Taos) is one of the most photographed churches in America. The adobe church initially started construction in the early to mid-1700s but took decades to complete, until 1816. The church is best known for its support system of massive adobe beehive buttresses. The rear of the mission is what you'll see most in paintings and photos (works of Ansel Adams and Georgia O'Keeffe included), but don't discount the beauty of the two bell towers in front. There's great light for photo opportunities both early and late in the day.

San Francisco de Asís is a designated National Historic Landmark and a United Nations Educational, Scientific, and Cultural Organization (UNESCO) World Heritage Site. The church has been restored traditionally over the years, taking painstaking effort to stay true to original techniques. The mission is also known for the art (retablos and santos) that hangs on its walls. The church is open year-round and the surrounding plaza has shops and food.

Top: San Francisco de Asís built in cruciform shape. Bottom, from left to right: colorful, hand-painted welcome sign on the small plaza; statue of St. Francis of Assisi inside the parish courtyard.

OTHER THINGS
to See and Do on the High Road to Taos

NAMBÉ PUEBLO LAKE AND FALLS

To reach the Nambé ranger station (from Santa Fe), travel north via US 84/285 to NM 503; turn east on NM 503 to the town of Nambé; then turn east onto Nambé Route 1. Nambé Pueblo Lake and Falls is open Thursday through Saturday from 7:00 a.m. to 7:00 p.m.; fees apply for activities as well as a small fee for cameras. Call (505) 455-2304 to confirm hours.

The Nambé Pueblo was founded in the fourteenth century and is a National Historic Landmark and a member of the Eight Northern Pueblos. As with so many pueblos, the Nambé went through significant changes after the Spanish conquistadors arrived, including the first church being built there in the 1600s. Unfortunately the original structure no longer stands for us to see. Today, visitors can enjoy their beautiful land of mountains highlighted with Nambé Falls and the reservoir. If you've got the time, plan to hike, picnic, trout fish, or even camp overnight. The hike to the falls makes for a great photo op, as do the petroglyphs along the river hike.

CORDOVA

After Chimayó, stay east on NM 76 to the village of Cordova, just 4 miles away. Before arriving, you'll come to a scenic pullout on the left of the highway.

Cordova is a small town is known for its artisan wood-carving industry. Thirty or so artists in Cordova are known as santeros, or those who make religious images. To purchase one of these artistic wood carvings, look for signs throughout town identifying where they are sold. These exquisite pieces of art are made primarily by artisans whose woodcarving skills have been passed down to them over generations. Pieces are made of aspen or cedar and can be expensive depending on the size.

TRUCHAS

From Chimayó, head north on NM 76 for 9 miles to reach Truchas.

Located 10 miles south of Trampas, this village is named for the Rio Truchas—"trout river." This remote enclave offers up impressive views of the Truchas Peaks, whose summits rise to 13,102 feet, 5,000 feet above

Truchas Peaks rise to a summit of 13,103 feet.

the town. Truchas may look familiar if you've seen Robert Redford's movie, *The Milagro Beanfield War*, which was filmed here in the '80s. There's an old mission in town that was finished in 1805 and has some of the oldest santero work found in New Mexico. The church of Nuestra Señora del Sagrado Rosario isn't open often (check ahead of time to plan your trip), but maybe you'll be lucky enough to go inside and view the gorgeous altar screens. Overall, the town hasn't changed much since it started as a Spanish land grant back in 1754. The roads are still narrow and the town still follows some of the land grant bylaws, like sharing the road with livestock. Traditional craftsmen still produce weavings, carvings, pottery, and more. The biggest change in this agricultural community is the addition of new artists and galleries.

PICURIS PUEBLO

Pueblo View, NM 75, Penasco, NM 87553
(575) 587-2519

It's a bit off the main road at the junction of NM 76 and NM 75 and sits alongside the Rio Pueblo.

The Picuris people participated in the Pueblo Revolt of 1680, fought

the Spanish in 1692, and then in 1706 fought with the Spanish against Indian tribes of the Apaches and Comanches. Today the Picuris is one of the smallest of the Tiwa pueblos. To envision all that went on in this area can be fascinating, especially to history buffs. Today, the old adobe church has been rebuilt, and there's a fishing pond for anglers and a small museum and shop with artwork by the local artists. Visitors can take a self-guided tour to see the grounds and unearthed historic dwellings. Take time to gaze at the strong beauty of the Picuris bison herd that they are proud to have back on tribal lands. There's a fee for entering the pueblo plus a photography fee if you want to snap pics. Anglers can acquire permits at the Picuris Pueblo Smoke Shop (1378 NM 75, Penasco, NM 87553) by calling (575) 587-2116, or through Picuris Pueblo Fish & Game and Parks & Wildlife by calling (575) 587-1601.

The Picuris are a federally recognized tribe who were given their name, Pikuria, meaning "those who paint," by Spanish explorer Don Juan de Oñate. This ancient tribe, who still create artistic pieces, is known to craft beautiful micaceous pottery from clay filled with glistening flecks of mica. Check their monthly calendar (picurispueblo.org/calendar-of-events-.html) for special events open to the public.

POT CREEK CULTURAL SITE

Southern Methodist University Campus in Taos
6580 NM 518, Ranchos de Taos, NM 87557
(505) 587-2255

From top to bottom: entrance sign to Pot Creek Cultural Site; entrance to ancient kiva dating back to 1100–1350 AD; Pueblo site of the Anasazi, the ancient ones.

Travel east on NM 75 and just past Vadito, then turn north (left) on NM 518. You'll be 15 miles from Penasco (about 6 miles from Taos,) when you will see the two signs and entrances leading into the site. Note that the gate to the parking lot will be locked, but you can park on the road and walk up.

Located in the Carson National Forest, this site is the ancient home of the Anasazi. Surprisingly, this site once had a pueblo with around four hundred rooms and other dwellings. Some research suggests it may be the earlier home of the Picuris and Taos Pueblo people as the site was abandoned around the same time the other two pueblos began. There's a mile loop to hike that begins on the far side of the parking area. Interpretive signs give historic information about the early inhabitants and lead to a kiva and pueblo site. The site is not officially open and is in stages of reconstruction, but visitation is allowed.

TALPA

Continuing from Pot Creek on NM 518, you'll reach Talpa in 5 miles.

Pit houses and pueblos built in Talpa date from 1100 to 1300 and this is where the Spanish settled in the early eighteenth century. Once named Rio Chiquito for the small creek that flows through it (which you can fish), this land grant village is now mostly just homes.

HIGH ROAD ART TOUR

highroadnewmexico.com
(888) 866-3643

Mark your calendar for the last two full weekends in September for the annual High Road Art Tour. The fall colors and scenery are breathtaking this time of year, and getting an opportunity to visit with so many artists and purchase their pieces right from where they work is particularly meaningful. While many of the artists along the High Road to Taos have their studios open year-round, some only open during this yearly tour. See firsthand the beauty of the land that inspires these artists and artisans from around the world.

LOW ROAD
TO TAOS

LOW ROAD TO TAOS
(THE RIVER ROAD)

From Santa Fe, the Low Road takes US 84/285 north to Española, then you'll bear right (northeast) and take NM 68 all the way to Taos. The Low Road is the newer highway that connects Santa Fe and Taos. It runs along the Rio Grande River and up the valley, and it, too, offers lovely, artful Spanish land grant villages nestled in amongst its curves. You will drive past lush valleys, mountains, and a long impressive canyon, go past river rafters and kayakers, past wineries and vineyards. You will have plenty of picturesque spots on the drive to stop and take photos.

The Low Road is a more direct route than the High Road to Taos and has fewer potential diversions. Driving the 70 miles from Downtown Santa Fe to Taos, expect to take an hour and a half if you don't stop a lot. Plan for more than that, because you'll find so much to stop for.

The gas station in Velarde is the only one between Española and Taos, so gas up before you go. The road is often curvy—slow down and enjoy the ride. Keep an eye out for wildlife at early morning, dusk, and night. Don't speed. Just follow alongside the fertile valley of the Rio Grande as it winds through a narrow canyon to the villages of Velarde, Embudo, Dixon, Rinconada, and Pilar.

Top: high-desert landscape along the Rio Grande River. Bottom, from left to right: artwork on an old building in Pilar; a bright fall view of the winding Rio Grande.

TASTE WINE AT LOCAL WINERIES

Black Mesa Winery
1502 NM 68, Velarde, NM 87582
(505) 852-2820
Hours: Monday–Saturday, 10:00 a.m.–6:00 p.m.;
        Sunday, noon–6:00 p.m.

Vivác Winery
2075 NM 68, Dixon NM 87527
(505) 579-4441
Hours: Monday–Saturday, 10:00 a.m.–6:00 p.m.; Sunday,
        noon–6:00 p.m.; extended summer hours

La Chiripada Winery and Vineyard
Hwy 75 CR 1119 #8, Dixon, NM 87527
(505) 579-4437 or (800) 528-7801
Hours: Monday, 11:00 a.m.–5:00 p.m.; Closed Tuesday;
        Wednesday–Saturday, 11:00 a.m.–5:00 p.m.;
        Sunday, noon–5:00 p.m.

Black Mesa Winery is located in Velarde, and you can see the vineyards out to your right. Enjoy their award-winning small-batch wines, handcrafted from New Mexico-grown grapes. Interestingly they have nearly three hundred petroglyphs on their property, so stay a little longer and hike around. (Note that they have a tasting room and wine bar in Taos as well, located at 241 Ledoux Street, Taos, NM 87571. Call (575) 758-1969 for their hours.)

La Chiripada and Vivác Wineries are located in Dixon along the Rio Embudo and NM 75 and around 25 miles south of Taos. Dixon is a creative town; vintners, organic farmers, and artists call this streamside village home. La Chiripada Winery and Vineyard has been crafting their award-winning wines for over thirty-five years, making them the oldest winery in New Mexico. (Their Taos tasting room is

Vivác tasting room in Dixon along the Low Road to Taos.

located at 103 Bent Street, Taos, NM 87571. Call (575) 751-1311 for their hours.) Vivác's handcrafted, boutique wines have an old-world style and their Estate Vineyards are all farmed organically. (Vivác also has a tasting room at 1607 Paseo De Peralta, Santa Fe, NM 87501.)

Call for details on tasting packages and enjoy this decades-long tradition of New Mexico wine inspired by old-world vintners, including the monks and Spaniards who settled here centuries ago.

Along this route, you will see orchards and roadside stands selling apples, peaches, cherries, and other locally grown fruits and vegetables. Take a moment to stop and feast on these freshly grown treats and grab a few extras to pair with your bottles of wine.

5 RAFT IN PILAR

From Dixon or Velarde,
go north on NM 68 to reach Pilar.

Pilar is a Spanish land grant settlement of Genizaro, people of mixed blood—lost tribes, who, when they were displaced by invaders, settled here. They were Spanish, Mexican, and Indian peoples in a forced diaspora. This settlement acted as a buffer zone from the attacks by Comanche and Apache, and was given by the King of Spain to these outcasts in the Cieneguilla Land Grant of 1793. The original name of the settlement was Cieneguilla (ciénega in Spanish means "marshy meadow"), named for a small flood plain here on the Rio Grande. This was a gathering spot for many years because of the flat land next to a good supply of year-round shallow water.

Pilar was renamed when the US took over in 1847. The postmaster could not spell Cieneguilla, so he renamed it Pilar after his wife. Pilar was a trading zone for many people. The inhabitants would gather mud from banks of Rio Grande and trade it at Picuris. The famous Battle of Cieneguilla also took place in Pilar in 1854, between the US Army and the Jicarilla Apache and Ute Indians.

Today Pilar and Orilla Verde Valley are home each year to thousands of rafters who splash and row down the Rio Grande. Many rafters and kayakers put in here around Pilar. Downstream are some great class 4 and 5 rapids to check out before you come to Velarde, which is the next logical stopping point. Pilar is also becoming an artist's community and there are several galleries around town.

After Pilar, NM 68 begins to climb up and out of the gorge into the valley. You'll soon be at the top of the horseshoe turn just south of Taos. This is a good time to stop to admire the expansive landscape of Taos Valley, see the great rift through which the Rio Grande rushes, and take time to look to the horizon where you will see Taos nestled against the mountains.

Beautiful October landscape highlights a fun rafting trip along the Rio Grande.

SIGHTSEE AT
TAOS JUNCTION BRIDGE

From Pilar, travel north on NM 570 and then turn right (east/northeast) onto NM 570. Drive about 2 miles to reach the monument and the Orilla Verde Recreation Area. NM 570 continues along the river, past accesses, campgrounds, and picnic places, for 6 miles before reaching Taos Junction Bridge.

Taos Junction Bridge is a small truss bridge over the Rio Grande River, just north of Pilar. Just below the bridge is a popular put-in spot for Rio Grande rafting or kayaking trips. The bridge is photogenic from below or above. If you cross the bridge, you are on the west side and can take NM 567 to the West Rim/Upper Rim Road (Road 115) and head north to Rio Grande Gorge Bridge.

Taos Junction Bridge is a popular locale for sightseeing, fly fishing, and hiking nearby.

From Pilar, take NM 68 north for 6.4 miles.
Taos Valley Overlook is located between mile markers 35
and 36 south of Taos. Recreationalists will find a
system of six interconnecting trails (over 20 miles).

The 2,600-acre Taos Valley Overlook sits on the rim of the gorge
above Taos Junction Bridge and the Orilla Verde Recreation Area. The
overlook section is all about non-motorized recreation, and that is why
you will find an interconnected system of hiking and mountain biking
trails (some for horseback riding) that gently move up and down
through sage, piñon, and rabbitbrush.

The overlook's views down into the gorge are exhilarating,
expansive, and impressive. You will find several trails that link up
with paths climbing from the river. The Taos Valley Overlook Trails
consist of several single-track loops and two track trails, totaling
about 16 miles with an intermediate level of difficulty.

SLIDE TRAIL

Distance: 2.5 miles round-trip
Elevation gain: 700 feet
Trailhead: You can come in on County Road 110 and park in the dirt
lot next to where the road was closed. You'll be able to see the trail.
If you are coming from the north from the Rio Grande Gorge Bridge,
head west on US 64 for 1 mile and turn left (south) on Taos County
Road CB 115 (Upper Rim Road). Continue for 8 miles and merge
with NM 567 E. Continue for 2.5 miles to Taos Junction Bridge. You
will cross Taos Junction Bridge and turn left into the Rio Pueblo
Campground.

At publication, the day-use fee was three dollars per car. You can
drive a short way up the road to the left and park near the trailhead.

If you are coming from the south from Taos Plaza, drive south
5 miles on Paseo del Pueblo Sur and turn right onto CR 110. Continue

5 miles where the road dead-ends at the new CR 110 trailhead. Travel another 4 miles. The road is paved up until almost the end where it turns to dirt. Here you'll find a dirt parking lot and the trailhead.

Some twenty years or so ago, we used to take the old NM 570 into Pueblo and it was always with trepidation because it was dicey, gravelly, steep, and way too close to the edge where a bad turn might land you in the Rio Pueblo. A basalt rock landslide closed it, and in turn it became a popular trail. The hike begins at the trailhead at river level on the Rio Pueblo de Taos and ascends steeply.

The big gray rocks look like elephants and rhinos and battleships. Keep an eye out for bighorn sheep, which are commonly sighted along the Rio Pueblo. On the Slide Trail you'll gain access to the whole area. Hike along the Slide Trail and you'll reach the confluence of the Rio Grande and the Rio Pueblo de Taos. Continue on to Taos Junction Bridge—that's where you find the lower trailhead.

WEST RIM TRAIL

Distance: 18 miles round-trip
Elevation gain: None, but you're at about 6,900 feet of elevation
Trailhead: There are two access points: The north trailhead is located at the rest stop on the west rim of the Rio Grande Gorge Bridge just off US 64. The south trailhead is located just off NM 567 at the north end of the Orilla Verde Recreation Area (see page 81).

This trail connects Taos Junction Bridge and Taos Valley Overlook to the north and Rio Grande Gorge Bridge. It also connects Low Bridge to High Bridge. This is an easy-to-moderate trail that meanders along the rim of the Rio Grande Gorge and down into the canyon.

PICURIS TRAIL

Distance: 1.5 miles round-trip

Elevation gain: 600 feet

Trailhead: Follow driving directions to Taos Junction Bridge (see page 76). The trail begins on the east side of the bridge.

This is a somewhat-difficult hike with awesome views that uses an old stock trail. There are connections to other trails in this section that allow for a longer hike.

RIFT VALLEY TRAIL AND TRADERS TRAIL

Distance: Rift Valley, 9 miles for the loop; Traders Trail, 3 miles round-trip

Elevation gain: So many trails intersect these trails, but if you follow it to its conclusion, you have a long, gradual descent to the gorge, 880 feet below.

Trailhead: Travel south on NM 68 from Taos and turn right (west) on CR 110. Stay on CR 110 for several miles until it ends. Park in the lot. The trail is on the south side of the lot.

East of the rim, you can hike or ride Traders Trail and Rift Valley, a loop that is ideal for novice hikers or bikers; you'll also find horseback riders and trail runners on these trails. Use the Traders Trail to get to the Rift Valley Trail. Traders Trail also connects to several other trails including Klauer, La Gijosa, and Anthony St. Armijo.

Local trails at Taos Valley Overlook lead outdoor enthusiasts to great views and adventures.

LA VISTA VERDE TRAIL

Distance: 2.5 miles round-trip

Elevation gain: Negligible

Trailhead: La Vista Verde Trail is located on NM 567, a half-mile above Taos Junction Bridge.

This is a pretty flat (only slightly rolling) hike and you get to see petroglyphs along the way. The BLM rangers provide guided hikes in summer, and if you choose that you won't miss any Indian rock art. Find the Rio Grande Gorge Visitor Center at 2873 NM 68, Embudo, NM 87531. You can reach the center at (575) 751-4899.

PETACA POINT TRAIL

Distance: 8 miles round-trip

Elevation gain: 180 feet

Trailhead: Located on NM 567 on mesa top above Taos Junction Bridge (see page 76).

This is an easy sunny hike, with sweeping views.

LA SENDA DEL MEDIO TRAIL

Distance: 5 miles round-trip

Elevation gain: 100 to 200 feet

Trailhead: Begins at Pilar Campground. To reach the campground, travel south on NM 68 from Taos, then west on NM 570, and travel 1 mile.

This hike follows the east side of Rio Grande and links Pilar, Rio Bravo, Arroyo Hondo, Lone Juniper, and Petaca Campgrounds. You will find good views of the gorge and river along this trail.

LAS MINAS TRAIL

Distance: 1 mile round-trip

Elevation gain: None

Trailhead: Trail begins at the Rio Grande Gorge Visitor Center at 2873 NM 68, Embudo, NM 87531. You can reach the center at (575) 751-4899.

An easy hike, this trail gives good views of the gorge.

OTHER THINGS
to See and Do on the Low Road to Taos

ORILLA VERDE RECREATION AREA

From Taos, travel south 22 miles on NM 68, then turn north on NM 570; travel 5 miles to the entrance of the Recreation Area.

Beginning just south of the village of Pilar and stretching several miles north, the Orilla Verde Recreation Area (fee per car) is public land along either side of the Rio Grande, used primarily as a put-in or haul-out for rafting, but you can camp at any number of campgrounds here as well. The Orilla Verde Recreation Area offers a variety of trails, ranging from the easy Las Minas Trail at the Rio Grande Gorge Visitor Center and the La Senda del Medio Trail at the Pilar Campground to more difficult trails that climb the gorge and overlook the Taos Valley.

The Orilla Verde Recreation Area boasts seven campgrounds, several picnic areas, and two group shelters located along the river, as well as several boat launches including one below Taos Junction Bridge.

The climate along the river is semiarid, but you will be amazed at how the plant and animal life changes from the rim to the river. The river in this section is known for some of the best trout fishing in the Southwest,

A beautiful view of the Rio Grande in the Orilla Verde Recreation Area.

with healthy populations of rainbow and brown trout as well as northern pike. Many of the trails start at the rim of the river and most are steep and challenging. In addition to getting to the river to fish or sightsee, you might also find ancient petroglyphs. The human history of this area reaches back at least fifteen thousand years, and each of those cultures have left their imprint on the landscape—from thousands-of-years-old hunting sites, to Pueblo, Ute, and Comanche petroglyphs dating back hundreds of years, to the sheep camps and abandoned homesteads of the early part of the twentieth century, to the present-day adobe homes powered with electricity and water.

Try the Vista Verde Trail for an easy walk with great views. The trailhead is on the other side of the river, half a mile up the hill from Taos Junction Bridge off the dirt road NM 567. The trail is 1.2 miles one-way along the west edge of the river; a little less than a half-mile out, look for a small arroyo with a few petroglyphs. You return by the same trail.

DIXON COOPERATIVE MARKET

215 NM 75, Dixon, NM 87527

(505) 579-9625

From Taos, take NM 68 south to NM 75 east and find the market.

Dixon has a fun and interesting artist's studio tour (email info@dixonarts.org for more information) as well as a nice farmers' market, but don't miss the Dixon Cooperative Market. The co-op is a grocery business owned by several hundred community members. The Dixon Farmers' Market begins most years in the third week of June. They are located in front of the Co-op Market in central Dixon every Wednesday from 3:30 p.m. to 6:30 p.m. They sell fresh produce in a lively setting, usually accompanied by live music.

The Enchanted Circle and Cinema

You might have several moments of déjà vu as you travel the Enchanted Circle, because so many of the places you'll visit have been in the movies. Nearly fifty movies, television shows, and documentaries, and numerous commercials have been filmed in this region. Actor Dennis Hopper fell in love with Taos when shooting the 1969 film *Easy Rider* and became one of its most famous residents.

Some of the most iconic movies had shooting locations in the Enchanted Circle. *Lonesome Dove* filmed much of its Montana scenes near Angel Fire. *Easy Rider*, *Butch Cassidy and the Sundance Kid*, and *Wild Hogs* had major shooting locations in and around the Enchanted Circle. In *Natural Born Killers*, Mickey and Mallory got married on the Rio Grande Gorge Bridge. *No Country for Old Men* also had a tense scene in the Plaza Hotel in Las Vegas, New Mexico. Other movies you might know that were filmed in the area include *Terminator Salvation*, *The Milagro Beanfield War*, *Missouri Breaks*, *Valley of the Sun*, *Twins*, *Seraphim Falls*, and many, many more. One of our favorite television series, *Longmire*, was also shot in and around the Enchanted Circle.

A scene from No Country for Old Men *was filmed at this stairway of the Plaza Hotel.*

FROM TAOS
TO QUESTA

TAOS

Route: From Santa Fe, head west on US 84/285 for 23 miles, and
then north on NM 68 for 45 miles before reaching Taos.

Elevation: 6,969 feet

Population: 5,763

Lay of the land: high desert, sagebrush, scrub oak,
Sangre de Cristo Mountains

Welcome to Taos, Bienvenidos, and Na-Tah-La-Wamah.

Taos is special. If you spend time here, we can and will agree on
that. That feeling of the village being special is predicated so much
upon what people see: the vigas and retablos, fuchsia sunsets and
Sangre de Cristo, river and gorge. But we suggest what makes Taos so
special, so magical, is not only the things we see but also what we feel,
that which we do not see. The light and the space between the light.

The light and the space between the light is the only way to
explain why so many artists, photographers, writers, painters,
sculptors, and musicians settled in this valley tucked into these
mountains. The original Spanish explorers named this mountain
range Sangre de Cristo, or Blood of Christ, for the way that light
illuminated the sides of the mountains in sanguine hues of red and
pink. Every artist or writer talks about how the light on the plateau,
in the canyon, off the adobe walls, bounces with a unique ray of color
and density, worth capturing with brush or pen.

We have heard visitors use these New Age words to describe
Taos over many years: spell, magic, aura, mystical. Most who
visit Taos fall under its spell. There is a certain patient pulse, an
undeniable rhythm, to Taos—the pace of life here, the people who
live here. Talk to Taoseños and before long, you will understand

*Left to right, top: Taos signs guide visitors; the bell entry to historic Mabel Dodge
Luhan House. Middle: the gated entrance of the Mabel Dodge Luhan House. Bottom:
a cultural performance in Taos Plaza; statue of St. Francis of Assisi in a Taos garden.*

they have this same duality: defiant but welcoming, protective but social, fierce but loving, traditional but progressive, proud but willing, sophisticated yet pastoral, multicultural but one. This is a weird place. It's physically so close to the rest of the world and yet so far away, so alike the world but so different, intentionally and unintentionally.

Let's get past the obvious reasons why so many people come to Taos. The village has fantastic weather year-round. Taos has the greatest sunsets, some days alive and brilliant, other days subtle and nostalgic. The scenery includes tall mountains, rushing rivers, wide plateaus, deep gorges. Recreationalists can choose from fishing, hiking, biking, ballooning, skiing, climbing, rafting, kayaking, and the list goes on and on.

Taos is one of the art centers of America. The food scene is hip but traditional, and you won't believe just how many great eateries of all kinds exist in a town this small. Taos knows how to do events and festivals. Other things that make Taos a tourist haven include: museums, galleries, historical sites, geography and geology, all things Native American, nearby world-class ski resort, superior fishing options in every direction, some of the best bike trails in the Southwest, hikes of every kind, walking tours

A shop for unique finds in Taos.

Galleries, museums, and shops are nestled behind the walls of historic buildings along Kit Carson Road.

including historic and ghostly, unique architecture, a million stores to shop, restaurants and coffeehouses and chocolatiers and bakeries, churches, breweries and wineries, national forests and monuments, and state parks. Everything is near to so much else and yet somehow seems insulated.

So much to do, but so little time to do it, which is why people keep coming back to Taos. This is a tiny, high-desert-mountain, Euro-Mexican-Indian-Bohemian village at Earth's end, comfortable in its own skin; it's a hip, weird, trendy, laid-back, homespun, multicultural, arid (except in monsoon season), foodie and organic-vegan nirvana, all with the purpose of diffusing time so that you don't know what day it is.

Any attempt to tell the history of Taos has to include the story of the Indians of this land—and it will be poorly done by one who is not accustomed to the oration from thousands of years. The history we briefly share starts with the people who lived here first, eventually settled in the thousand-year-old sacred Taos Pueblo; then discusses the Hispanic heritage that informs the food, the architecture, and the customs; explores how the men and women of the Old West gave us

Mountain Biking around Taos

There are several mountain biking trails in the areas including Cebolla Mesa, Dunn Bridge, Gallina Creek, Ojitos, Garcia Park, Maestas Ridge, Picuris Mountains, Bernadin Lake, Gallegos Peak, Amole Canyon and West Rim Trail, but these are our picks.

South Boundary Trail: A popular and classic cross-country bike ride, some think this is the top ride in the state. The 20-mile trek takes you on a single-track through many types of landscape, everything from meadows and aspen glades, through conifer forests, past several peaks, and across ridges. You will have some technical challenges toward the end of the ride. There are claims that the length is 22 or 25 miles, but it's at least 20 miles, a very long day, and since it's one way you'll need a shuttle. Some say that it's best to let the shuttle take you to the Angel Fire side and ride back to Taos. Either way, this is a strenuous ride so take lots of water and snacks and a rain jacket, and be prepared to find cover from lightning since you'll be in high country.

The trail is best for intermediate and advanced riders. This is a great fall ride with lots of color from the aspen stands. The trail traverses the boundary of Carson National Forest from Angel Fire to Taos.

Another popular route is to start in Valle Escondido in Taos Canyon and ride up the road to Garcia Park and down from there.

Devisadero Peak Loop Trail: Located 4 miles southeast of Taos on US 64 at the edge of Rio Fernando de Taos Canyon. Park in the El Nogal parking lot and cross US 64 to access the trailhead. Popular, advanced single-track, 5-mile loop trail through juniper and piñon that's tight and rocky, steep and loose. This trail can be ridden in both directions.

myths to go along with true and often violent stories; and finally considers those who influenced Taos to become the birthplace of the Western Art movement in the early 1900s.

The Taos Valley has been a major trade and travel route as long as humans have been present in the area, from the Indians nearly ten thousand years ago to the development of the Santa Fe Trail in the nineteenth century. The first permanent inhabitants of Taos Valley were the Anasazi, the Pueblo people, beginning in 100 AD. They built multi-story complexes in a sophisticated familial community, and many believe the Taos Pueblo was constructed in the late 1300s or early 1400s in this same efficient, organizational design.

The story goes that the Taos Indians moved here a thousand or more years ago because a great eagle led them to this valley. They live here and are a part of the land and culture and people still today. When they met the Spanish conquistadors in the mid-1500s, the colonization and Christianization of the native people followed a familiar pattern we have seen in the West. The Spanish built mission churches, settlements were built along water, trading posts were established, trappers and mountain men found fertile lands for their ways, and pioneers began

Taos frequently has festivals and events in the Taos Plaza.

to establish farms and small communities. The Taos Indians grew more and more resistant to the impositions of the Spanish government and the Catholic church, and to the increasing needs and demands of the growing settlements of the Taos region.

Don Fernando de Taos was established in 1615 as an outpost of New Spain, its northernmost colony. Spain controlled Mexico, which was the major influencer of the Southwest. This outpost was the genesis of the Taos we know today. To provide context, Europeans landed in Plymouth Rock five years after the Taos settlement began. There was a peaceful coexistence between the Spanish, Mexicans, Anglos, and Taos Indians, with trading taking place and an agreement of defense against Apache, Navajo, and Ute attacks. All was going well until the great Pueblo Rebellion of 1680 when the Taos Indians expelled the settlers. A decade or two later, the Indians and settlers slowly worked out their differences and the settlers returned.

Fast forward about a hundred years wherein the Mexicans, Anglos, and Taos Indians began to cooperate and learn from each other, build houses, grow more crops, trade with more peoples and areas, and create an identity. It was from this period that you see the architecture that stands today, or was imitated in the Pueblo Revival architecture from the early twentieth century, the religious art with its santos and retablos and altars found in the churches. The Spanish continued to build settlements, give land grants, and build churches. So many of the churches you will visit during your Enchanted Circle tour were built during this time—the San Francisco de Asís church (see page 62) and the mission churches at Truchas and Trampas.

The Mexican, Indian, Anglos, and Spanish flourished in trading not only furs, mud, water, and protection but in cultural sharing. To the valley, Hispanos brought fruits, vegetables, and livestock, along with acequias to irrigate to the crops. The Pueblos showed the others how cook using adobe horno ovens, while the Spanish showed the people of the valley how to create buildings and homes with mud and timber and how to design communities around a central gathering place or plaza.

Commercial trading grew through annual trade fairs and made Taos a trading center among Mexicans, the French fur traders, mountain men, and various Indian tribes. Taos offered drink and food, communion and friendship, and song and dance that these people didn't get throughout their isolation. Mexico gained independence from Spain in 1821, eleven years after Father Hidalgo cried "Grito de Dolores" ("Cry of Dolores," said in the town of Dolores against colonial rule) and Taos and the surrounding areas were no longer part of New Spain. Mexico ruled passively with poor administration over the region for a quarter century but they had other things at home to worry about. A militarily unprepared Mexico was no match for a land-hungry America under expansionist President James K. Polk, and when the War with Mexico was over (1845–48), Mexico had lost about one-third of its territory, including nearly all of present-day California, Utah, Nevada, Arizona, and New Mexico. That opened the door for the United States to make this region part of the imposition and of its manifest destiny—and, as a result, part of its exploitation.

America sent out West its outcasts, wagon pioneers, disenfranchised, outlaws, runaways, land grabbers, and opportunists,

Transportation

Taos is a great place for public transportation and operates buses through the North Central Regional Transit District. The TSV Green Line operates from December 20 to March 30 and transports folks from town to the ski valley for free. They also operate free service to El Prado, Arroyo Seco, and Valdez. The Chile Red line provides free rides Monday through Friday throughout Taos.

The blue Taos Express bus is known for its weekend service (for a small fee) between Taos and Santa Fe, including Española. Make reservations for this line ahead of time.

Check out their schedules for all the details on times and pick-up and drop-off stops at ncrtd.org/taos-area.aspx, or call (866) 206-0754.

and most importantly its system of justice and its armed forces. No longer was the Catholic Church the most important influencer.

Railroads were built to connect the world of the East to the ever-growing colonies in the West. Mining, farming, and cattle led more people to the region, and with them the American settlers brought their disrespect for customs and traditions and, most importantly, their greed. The tension grew between the indigenous cultures and the European cultures, and rebellion became inevitable. The native peoples resisted the excessive forceful changes. The New Mexico territory's first governor, Charles Bent, issued a proclamation, and in response the local Indians rebelled in what is called the Pueblo Revolt of 1847. Bent was killed and scalped by protesting Pueblo Indians and settlers who feared that the new ways would cost them their land and means of existence. In response, the US cavalry came and forcefully squashed the rebellion.

After the revolt, artists and writers started appearing in the Taos village, and when mining started up at Twining (now Taos Ski Valley) in the 1870s and '80s, Taos was peaceful, settled, and ready for the influx of artists over the next forty years. You will find mentions throughout Taos of Joseph Henry Sharp, Irving Couse, Ernest Hennings, Walter Ufer, and Victor Higgins. The East found this region of the Southwest intriguing. In 1898 young artists Bert Phillips and Ernest Blumenschein discovered Taos Valley after their wagon broke down just north of the area. They loved what they found and stayed, and with other like-minded artists they began a tradition of art and beauty that exists today.

In 1915, six artists formed the Taos Society of Artists, known as the Taos Six. Subsequently, other artists, writers, and intellectuals such as Mabel Dodge Luhan, D.H. Lawrence, and Georgia O'Keeffe joined this thriving Taos scene. They saw the Light, so to speak. Today, you can hardly turn around without finding an amazing art gallery, or an artist, sculptor, or writer. The tradition and patronage of the arts is alive and well.

When Dennis Hopper and the production crew of the movie *Easy Rider* came to town to shoot in the late 1960s, the influence of that art movement, of the movie, and of the welcoming laid-back vibe of Taos, brought hippies and their creative bohemian lifestyle to the area. Hopper loved Taos so much that he made it his second home. He brought many of his Hollywood friends but also sculptors, photographers, painters, and other artists, and you can still find their work, or the artists themselves, in Taos today. This ushered in the New Age influence on Taos.

Taos is home to more than twenty sites on the National Register of Historic Places. The village is a tiny, but big, place where tourism is king, lodging is expensive, real estate even more so, and almost every restaurant is great. Even today you can see the historical influences all around Taos, from the Taos Indians, conquistadores, French fur-traders, mountain men, Mexican settlers, American pioneers, artists and writers, and hippies and outdoors people. Even as Taos moves toward tourism, it continues to look to define what it is and wants to be.

Taos has a lot of traffic for a small town, especially at lunch and the end of the work day, and again when there's something big going on at the plaza or park. So that's a big negative. Some locals will say there's too much progress. We've

From top to bottom: shoppers explore the stores of John Dunn; a handmade sign for psychic readings around Taos; artists' cooperative filled with a variety of mediums and styles of art.

been coming here for thirty-five years, and not all that much has changed. The more it changes, the more it stays the same. It's all a matter of perspective. Taos is still small, laid-back, quaint, quirky, unique, and weird—a melding of so many cultures. Tourism drives most things in Taos, and artists, galleries, outfitters, and retail businesses are generally designed to please tourists. Tourists can find every level of lodging, from hotels and

Art and locally sourced finds are special draws for those who come to Taos.

motels to bed and breakfasts and cabins to casitas and condos. Taos has become one of the premier vacation destinations in the Southwest.

Taos remains the center of the Northern New Mexico region, the centerpiece of the Enchanted Circle. The village is intimate, and when you return Taos will feel nostalgic, the same each time you visit, memorable for what you had together; yet Taos is different each time too, and on those days, you will forge new experiences and memories, see new light and the space between the light.

Never have we been anywhere in the world (and we have traveled the world) where you see disparate cultures coming together so seamlessly, familiarly, happily. To top it off, it all takes place in such a gorgeous, wild place that's metaphorical in many ways—the duality of forested mountains meeting a great rifted plain. Let the light shine.

Keep Taos weird.

Insider Tips & Information about Taos

- Watch out for intense UV rays and use sunblock and a hat or cap.
- Be ready for a weather change. If you wait a little bit, it will happen.
- Be aware that in any elevation climb that you might get out of breath. You don't want to get altitude sickness (see page 21).
- If you think you might have to soak your feet in a river or hot springs, bring a change of shoes. Carry a pair of Tevas or Chacos to get that Taos foot tan!
- Wait at crosswalks for cars to stop. It's a state law for them to do so, but there might be an out-of-towner who doesn't know the law, so be alert.
- Walking is better than driving in many cases because of traffic and parking. Even when walking, watch out because the streets are narrow and uneven—so hold on to your older or wobbly loved ones.
- Bikes are tough to ride safely in Taos if you ask us, what with narrow streets, lots of traffic, uneven sidewalks, and unaware pedestrians. But if you do decide to go with a bike, be safe.
- You'll be surprised there are so many restaurants in a town this small and how many are of such high-quality, big-city level. There are so many choices of genre, cost, and quality.
- Taos enjoys its outdoor eating areas and many places have them. It's also a very dog-friendly place, and many cafés and shops will have water bowls outside for your dogs and even allow them on their patios.
- It's a very international place. As you walk around, you'll hear different languages.
- La Fonda means "boarding house" in Spanish.
- Taos is derived from the indigenous word for "red willow" because the Taos Indians were known as the Red Willow people (Red Willow Creek runs through the land).

Christmas in Taos

Annual Lighting of the Trees: In early December, Taos Plaza is set aglow with Christmas lights, caroling, performers, electric light parade, Grinch sightings, and appearances by Santa and Mrs. Claus.

Lighting of Ledoux: In early December, enjoy a caroling procession from Taos Plaza guides Father Winter up Ledoux; includes bonfires, cookies and punch, wine sipping, and touring of the Harwood Museum. This is a local, charming start to Christmas (see Ledoux Street on page 101 for more).

Bonfires on Bent Street: In early December, join a block party throughout The Shops at John Dunn area, including warming bonfires scattered all around, free posole and warm drinks, music, and festivities.

Las Posadas: These cultural Christmas celebrations last nine days, December 16–24, ending on the 24th with Midnight Mass at San Francisco de Asís. Posadas is the traditional play which tells the story of Mary and Joseph looking for lodging before baby Jesus was born.

New Year's Eve on Taos Plaza: A family-friendly, alcohol-free evening of food, live music, impressive balloon launch and fireworks display. This ends early, so if you want to have an official countdown with spirits you can do both.

The Taos Pueblo and Picuris Pueblo: Both pueblos have annual events and feast days throughout the year so be sure to check their calendars (taospueblo.com/category/calendar/ and picurispueblo.org/calendar-of-events-.html), including events at Taos Pueblo on Christmas Eve, Procession of the Virgin Mary, and the Taos Pueblo Deer or Matachinas Dance on Christmas Day—a symbol of abundance in winter.

Visit taos.org/events/festivals/yuletide-in-taos/ for more information on these events.

Left: a giant Christmas tree in Taos Plaza. Right, from top to bottom: bonfire on Ledoux during Yuletide; luminarias, or farolitos, line a doorway during the Christmas season; Santa makes his appearance at the Lighting of Ledoux.

8 TOUR THE HACIENDA DE LOS MARTINEZ

708 Hacienda Road, Taos, NM 87571
(575) 758-1000
The Martinez Hacienda is a short drive from the Taos Plaza.
Drive along Paseo Del Pueblo Sur (south) to NM 240, turn
right, and in about 2 miles turn right on Hacienda Road.

Hacienda de los Martinez, built on the banks of the Rio Pueblo de
Taos, stands as one of the country's few remaining Spanish colonial
haciendas. Don Antonio Severino Martinez settled here in 1804 and
began building his family home, which grew from four to twenty-one
rooms. The fortress-styled hacienda has two courtyards and was built
with thick adobe walls for protection from the Plains Indian tribes.

The Martinez family worked on their ranch and farm and had
several Native American servants who helped in the operation of
farming and ranching as well as with weaving and knitting. Their

Preserved places like Hacienda de los Martinez teach us about Taos's past.

hacienda was the last stop along the famed El Camino Real, the Spanish trade route connecting New Mexico and Mexico City. Now owned by the Taos Historic Museums, the property is on the National Register of Historic Places and considered a living museum.

The Martinez's eldest son became the famed Padre Martinez, who deeply believed in upholding the Hispanic nature of the Catholic church in the area and battled against Bishop Lamy to do so. Padre Martinez continued his influence in Taos by starting a school and bringing the first printing press to town.

This historical locale offers an easy-to-follow, self-guided tour that takes about an hour. The hacienda is packed with artifacts and displays showing what life was like here in the nineteenth century. They offer lots of special exhibits and demonstrations throughout the year, so be sure to check their calendar of events on taoshistoricmuseums.org/.

Take an extra hour or two out of your schedule to pay this unique piece of history a visit. Admission is under ten dollars and well worth it.

WALK LEDOUX STREET

9

Taos's historic Ledoux Street lies within walking distance from the plaza. Ledoux is a short little street, tucked away and relatively easy to miss since it's off the main road and not directly connected to the plaza. Look for the historical marker, near the painted horses mural, on the eastern end of the street to begin your journey along Ledoux. The best way to navigate Ledoux is by foot as it's quite narrow.

Ledoux was once secured with gates at each end in a fortress style for protection. Outside walls of homes were connected for protection from Indian attacks and give Ledoux that charming, snuggled-in feel that it has today.

Ledoux Street is named for a French-Canadian fur trader, Antoine Ledoux, who settled here around 1844 when fur trade was big business. But this block had a history before its namesake with the likes of

another Canadian fur trader, Charles Beaubien, who created a Taos
history for himself and whose son was killed during the Taos Revolt
of 1847, and with Smith H. Simpson, whose family ended up selling
a portion of the land on Ledoux to the Harwoods, leading to today's
notable Harwood Museum of Art. Ledoux became Taos's first art district
and today is still recognized as the heart of the town's art district.

Two young artists started their love affair with Taos in 1898 when
they ended up stranded outside of town due to a broken wagon
wheel. Trying to get from Denver to Mexico, Ernest Blumenschein
and Bert Phillips tossed a coin to see who would lug their broken
wheel 20 miles into Taos. Blumenschein lost the toss, but they both
won when they realized what a jewel of place they had found in this
creative town. Their affinity for Taos spread, and other artists joined
them in this beautiful, captivating country. In a few short years, the
famed Taos Society of Artists was formed.

Blumenschein and his wife, Mary Greene Blumenschein, also
an artist, moved into an old fortress-style adobe home on Ledoux
street in 1919. They ended up purchasing other connecting homes and

The galloping horses mural on historic Ledoux.

built doors to join them, creating a sprawling piece of property along Ledoux. Today the Blumenschein Home and Museum (222 Ledoux Street, Taos, NM 87571) allows visitors to get a good peek into the lives of some of Taos's notable artists. Visitors will see art from the Blumenschein family as well as pieces from other Taos Society artists. The house is still furnished, so you'll get an authentic feel of what Blumenschein's life was like here on Ledoux.

End your Ledoux tour at the Harwood Museum of the University of New Mexico (238 Ledoux Street, Taos, NM 87571). It's small but is considered a cultural center filled with art of the Taos region. Of course the Taos Society of Artists have paintings here in addition to exhibits including Native American art, Hispanic tradition, Taos modern art, and more. As a research center, the Harwood Museum has collected thousands of old photographs as well as letters and drawings related to this region. Check the Harwood calendar at harwoodmuseum.org/ for special exhibits, and be sure to investigate the gift shop too.

As you wind through Ledoux's thoroughfare, take time to soak in the historic beauty of the adobe walls and colorful doors, the flowers and sage, the artists' hideaways and their creations. Imagine being gated in for safety during a time of conflicting cultures, fur trade, and exploration. Imagine life on Ledoux, then and now. Ledoux may be small, but it has a history to tell. Now if its walls could only talk.

Lighting of Ledoux takes place at the beginning of December as a celebration of light to start the wintertime, holiday season, or Yuletide, as it's known in Taos. Locals come out to sing carols and stroll Ledoux while escorting Father Winter from the plaza all the way to the Harwood Museum, which is open for the evening. Hundreds of traditional farolitos line the street and tops of buildings. Firepits are scattered along the way and people huddle and cheer the season. It's a beautiful, peaceful time on Ledoux.

10 EXPLORE TAOS PLAZA AND TAOS DOWNTOWN HISTORIC DISTRICT

The Taos Plaza is located at the intersection of Kit Carson Road and Paseo de Pueblo in the middle of Taos.

The heart of Taos lies in the middle of downtown in the Taos Plaza, which is three hundred years old and marks the end of the famous El Camino Real. The Don Fernando de Taos Plaza is the gathering spot—a relaxing place to meet friends, grab a coffee, leisurely shop, visit an art gallery, eat local cuisine, rest your bones, purchase fresh vegetables at market, listen to local musicians, or join in with hundreds of others at one of numerous festivals and events held throughout the year.

If you use the Taos Plaza as a home base, you are within walking distance from even more shopping, restaurants, art galleries and much more. If you travel the Enchanted Circle Scenic Byway, you simply must factor in a few hours to visit this lovely Spanish-colonial traditional town square. You might get lucky and see a traditional celebration or a live musical performance. If you can't find parking in the plaza—and mind you, during the week you have active parking meters—you can find parking on the nearby streets, at the John Dunn Shops parking lot, west across North Plaza Street, behind the plaza on the other side of Camino de Santa Fe, and on Dona Luz Street, along Paseo del Pueblo Norte, or even in Kit Carson Park.

The Taos Plaza was built like many Spanish settlements in northern New Mexico, with low adobe buildings and houses surrounded by a fortified wall for protection against Indian attacks. The outside of any building would not have had windows. The settlement had towers to watch for intruders and the plaza was gated.

The plaza has seen many changes over the years. Few original buildings still exist due to reconstruction, fires, and progress, although the architectural spirit and style from the original buildings remain. Many of the buildings in the area mimic the style of those constructed in the 1800s. The courthouse used to be on the plaza. The plaza had an extensive renovation in the 1970s.

The Taos Plaza is on the National Register of Historic Places. Almost every building in and around the plaza falls in the Downtown Historic District. The La Fonda Hotel building still stands tall and proud on the south side of the plaza since its inception back in 1820. It's had different owners, and one was a D.H. Lawrence fan who purchased a collection of his controversial paintings that is still housed at the hotel. The collection is under lock and key, but visitors can take a look for a small fee. Just check with the hotel's front desk clerk.

Hotel La Fonda, Spanish for "The Inn," began as a mercantile that rented rooms.

Taos Walking Tour

Taos is small enough that you can walk around town to see a number of its historical highlights. The Taos self-guided walking tour is a great place to start for the crux of what the downtown's center has to offer. You can download the exact tour at Taos.org, but many of the places within walking distance from the plaza hold much of the town's history.

The downloadable brochure will give you the lowdown on each landmark in relation to Taos's past. Start out at the two-hundred-year-old plaza in the center of town, and explore from there. Take caution walking as there may be uneven spots and steps along the way. If you park your car in the plaza, bring coins for the parking meters.

Walking up Ledoux will lead you to several of the other highlighted spots, including the Blumenschein House and the Harwood Museum.

All of the locales on the map are fairly close together, so you will be able to see the sights easily. Taos has such a rich, diverse past with so many levels of change and growth that it's a history lover's dream to explore.

If you'd rather take a guided tour, check with the visitor center at 1139 Paseo del Pueblo Sur, Taos, NM 87571, or call (575) 758-3873) for details. Tour companies provide a number of touring options from a trolley tour to a walking exploration of the ghosts of Taos's past. Other walking tours include scoping out Taos's architectural styles including Mission Revival of the Historic Taos Inn, Territorial Style of the Kit Carson Home and Museum, and Spanish Pueblo Revival of the Harwood Museum and the Mabel Dodge Luhan House. A walking tour can also specifically focus on the homes and studios of the Taos Society of Artists' ten most prominent members.

SHOP AT THE FARMERS MARKET

Located at Taos Plaza, the Farmers Market opens the
second Saturday of May, from 8:00 a.m. to 12:30 p.m.,
and is open each Saturday until it gets too cold,
around late October or early November.

This is a must-do. Taos Farmers Market Saturdays are a tapestry of color and food, locals and tourists, smells and sounds, vibrancy and calm. Get to Farmers Market on Saturday morning and don't be in a rush. Bring a reusable bag, or, better yet, a handmade woven basket-bag. Buy some local veggies and fruits, eat a Taos-inspired street-food breakfast (scone, empanada, or green chile and chorizo burrito, anyone?), get a custom poem written just for you (typed on a manual typewriter, no less), try some freshly roasted chiles, listen to local musicians, and get to know Taos in a way that is more intimate than any other. The Farmers Market is a colorful, tasty collection of things grown by local farmers: piñon nuts, carrots, onions, lettuces, herbs, tomatoes, cacti, turnips, cherries, peaches, mushrooms, plums, radishes, all kinds of pretty flowers, and so much more. Sensory overload.

Taos Farmers Market, the place to be during the warm months and early fall.

VIEW THE KIT CARSON HOUSE AND MUSEUM

113 Kit Carson Road, Taos, NM 87571
(575) 758-4945
Located just off the plaza, near center of town, on
Kit Carson Road (NM 68), this National Historical Landmark
is just a short walk south from the plaza.

Another must do! The territorial-style adobe home was built in 1825 and has been lovingly preserved. Kit Carson is probably the most famous pioneer in American history, and for good reason. He was a fur trapper, guide, Indian agent, US Army Officer, and all-around mountain man. He was so revered and famous, his exploits so exaggerated, that he was featured in dime novels in his own lifetime and was a living legend. He lived among Indians, married into the Arapaho and Cheyenne tribes, fought in numerous battles including the Civil War, mapped and explored entire regions of the West. He married three times and fathered ten children. He lived in Taos much of his adult life but died at Fort Lyon, Colorado, in 1868.

The hornos, an adobe outdoor oven, at the Kit Carson House and Museum.

The home is a great example of the Spanish Colonial homes of the nineteenth century: central courtyard, horseshoe-shaped design, and a long territorial building with thick walls, small rooms, low ceilings, and low doorframes.

In the courtyard you'll find an outdoor oven, called a horno, which is used in summer so the heat didn't make the house unbearable. You'll also find lots of great wall hangings (photos, memorabilia, etc.) and period staging to make it look like it would during Carson's life. The museum is small and doesn't take long to tour even if you take time to watch the video about Kit Carson, which is well worth it.

The museum attracts twenty thousand visitors a year. The gift shop has lots of books on local, New Mexican, and Southwestern history you won't find elsewhere.

DINE AT THE HISTORIC TAOS INN AND ADOBE BAR 13

125 Paseo Del Pueblo Norte, Taos, NM 87571
(575) 758-2233
It takes less than five minutes to walk from
the plaza to the inn, located in four buildings.

You'll know this inn by the landmark thunderbird sign keeping sentinel over Paseo del Pueblo Norte, just across from the intersection with Bent Street, a block north of the plaza. It's blue and white during the day and lit up with pink neon at night. The legendary Historic Taos Inn began as the private residence of Taos's first and only doctor at the time, Doc Martin, back in the 1890s. Doc Martin's wife Helen was an artist, and it was in this home that the famed Taos Society of Artists was formed. Doc and Helen purchased other adobe homes adjacent to theirs and surrounding the small plaza that was once Taos's first downtown area. They rented the homes to writers and artists of the time.

Upon Doc's death and the unrelated burning of a Taos hotel in

The Taos Inn is a popular stop for dining, lodging, listening to music and having a drink, or photographing the sign.

1936, Helen purchased the last home on the small plaza and turned her collection of houses into Hotel Martin. That plaza is now the Taos Inn's quaint two-story lobby, and the last home Helen purchased is now the adjoining Adobe Bar. In total, the houses making up the hotel stretch nearly a block along Taos's main thoroughfare, Paseo del Pueblo Norte.

Back in the day, the hotel was considered a creative and intellectual social center. Today the inn honors that time and continues artistic inspiration by hosting art series, exhibits, and festivals.

The Taos Inn sits in the heart of the town's historic district and is filled with charm and history. It's been touted as one of the great inns in the country and even has some star power to back it up. Famous folks like Greta Garbo, Pawnee Bill, Robert Redford, and Jessica Lange have all walked through these doors.

The Adobe Bar serves up good noshing food, nice pours, tasty margaritas, and more, while Doc Martin's restaurant is known for an extensive wine list and high-quality menu items. The lobby, known as Taos's living room, and the outside porch are great people-watching spots and are generally quite crowded. There's live music in the lobby every night of the week, so get there early for a prime spot as it's a small intimate space. You never know when an unexpected entertainer will pop in and perform, as Billy Corgan of the Smashing Pumpkins has done.

Whether you're spending the evening or the whole night, or just grabbing a cold drink, take a moment to soak in the history and undeniable charm of this prime Taos locale.

VISIT THE GOVERNOR BENT HOUSE AND MUSEUM

14

117 Bent Street, Taos, NM 87571
(505) 758-2376

The museum is located in the home of Charles Bent, the first governor of New Mexico, who was murdered by an angry mob in 1847. You'll find inside an interesting mix of Governor Bent–related things, nineteenth-century artifacts of the area, and works of Taos artists. This small, quirky museum might not rival the bigger, more complete museums, but it has its own kind of charm.

Bent, his brother William, and Ceran St. Vrain built Bent's Fort in Colorado, a successful and well-known trading post visited by pioneers, mountain men, and Indians. Bent turned his fame and contacts into an appointment to the governorship in 1834. Protest by Mexican and Pueblo Indians was in the air in 1846–47 and Bent knew that he needed to quell it before things got serious. He traveled from Santa Fe to Taos in mid-January. A mob gathered, and after murdering the sheriff the Indians moved over to Governor Bent's

The Governor Bent House and Museum is a quirky museum that's tucked away in Taos. Don't miss it.

Taos Hum

Sometime in the early 1990s, some people started reporting hearing a hum in Taos. Most people locate it west of Taos near Tres Orejas. Does it really exist? Scientists have studied the hum and report that: 1) only 2 percent of people can discern the hum at all, and 2) there is no evident reason for the hum and no evidence that it actually exists. But if you like the supernatural or psychological, listen up and see if you are one of the chosen.

house. He tried to calm them but he was shot by gun and arrow, and was killed and scalped right in front of his door.

A great book to purchase if you want to know all the details about the Revolt of 1847 is *Tragedy in Taos: The Revolt of 1847*, by James A. Crutchfield. The ensuing tragic events helped shape the region. The Bent House is located one block north of the plaza and one half-block west of the Taos Inn on Bent Street.

15 PICNIC IN THE KIT CARSON PARK AND HISTORIC CEMETERY

211 Paseo Del Pueblo Norte, Taos, NM 87571
(575) 751-2001
The park is located one and a half blocks
north of Taos Plaza.

Over 150 years old, this park is one of the main gathering places for events, festivals, markets, fairs, concerts, and general park activities.

The cemetery houses the graves of several historical figures, the most famous being Kit Carson and his wife, Josephine, but also including Padre Martinez and other prominent Taoseños. The big music concerts in Taos are held here, including the Taos Solar Music Festival; Mumford and Sons and Alabama Shakes have also played here. In addition, the town recently started hosting Movies on the Green, a summertime family event.

Oftentimes tents are set up for arts and crafts fairs and various events. There are lots of trees, open fields, tennis, basketball, and sand volleyball courts, picnic and grill areas, a playground for children, and fields for soccer, frisbee, and baseball. It is also a great place for a getaway to picnic

The small historical cemetery in Kit Carson Park, home to some of Taos's famous folks of the past.

on some local cheese and wine and enjoy the mountain vistas. This twenty-five-acre park features a three-quarter-mile walking and jogging track around the perimeter. The cemetery and park are both ADA accessible.

VIEW ART AT THE FECHIN HOUSE 16

227 Paseo del Pueblo Norte, Taos, NM 87571
(575) 758-2690
Also the location of the Taos Art Museum, the Fechin House is a quarter-mile north of the Taos Plaza.

If you don't reach the Nicolai Fechin House on the Taos Walking Tour, then take time to stop by on your way out of Taos. Today the Fechin House is the home of the Taos Art Museum, but it was once the place Russian artist Nicolai Fechin called home. Fechin was born in 1881 and landed in Taos after leaving his homeland due to struggles after World War I. He came here in his forties by way of New York and visited Mabel Dodge Luhan, who had quite the influence on convincing artists and creators to move to Taos.

Artist Nicoli Fechin's former home and the current Taos Art Museum.

Fechin purchased this two-story adobe in 1928 and spent time artistically remodeling and carving fittings and furniture influenced by Russian design along with elements of his new Southwestern locale. He came by his artistic skills naturally under the tutelage of his craftsman father, who was skilled with wood and metalworking and who also introduced Fechin to drawing and sculpting. Nicolai Fechin spent his life painting and studying, and is now known as one of the top portrait artists of the twentieth century. He completed a number of works during his time in Taos from portraits of Native Americans to the hard-to-resist New Mexico landscape.

Many of his creations, and those of others from his time period, are on display in the Taos Art Museum, his former home. Fechin lived in Taos for only six years, but his creative touch continues to inspire others. Even after a divorce, his home remained in the family, from his wife to his daughter and finally to his granddaughter who made the sale leading to the museum we know today. Get the rest of the story by visiting the Fechin House and exploring the museum.

GET INSPIRED AT THE MABEL DODGE LUHAN HOUSE

17

240 Morada Lane, Taos, NM 87571
(800) 846-2235 or (575) 751-9686
Two blocks east from Taos Plaza on Kit Carson Road,
turn left (north) on Morada Lane to reach the
paved road for the Mabel Dodge Luhan House.

Tucked away on a quiet road not too far from the Taos Plaza, and still within walking distance, Mabel's home is now an historic inn and conference center.

Mabel was a character and wealthy socialite from New York who was known in the arts and social communities of New York and Europe. She came to Taos seeking fulfillment and to attract intellectuals and

A hidden gem, the Mabel Dodge Luhan House.

creative types to commiserate and share in her new fascination of this Southwest locale. As her support of the arts continued in Taos, she hosted artists, thinkers, and creators in her adobe home shared with her fourth husband, Tony Luhan, from the Taos Pueblo.

Her house boasts an interesting history. It drew all sorts of interesting visitors to its salon atmosphere. Some came for inspiration, personal growth, or for a retreat. Names like Willa Cather, Ansel Adams, D.H. Lawrence, and Georgia O'Keeffe were inspired here. There are lots of stories of the goings-on at the Luhan house. Years later, the home was purchased by actor Dennis Hopper, who continued the salon atmosphere of entertaining and socializing.

Come visit and get inspired yourself at Mabel Dodge Luhan's home. You don't have to stay the night to poke around and feel the inspiration.

Looking for Something Different to Do in Taos?

- Check out the murals inside the Old County Courthouse.
- Take a tour of the area's wineries and breweries.
- Eat regional food. If you already like New Mexican food, stretch out of your comfort zone and eat something local you've never tried (like green chiles in your beer).
- Hire a guide for a haunted tour of Taos.
- Time a trip to coincide with a Taos festival or event.
- Go on a llama trek with a local outfitter.
- Reserve a trip for the Christmas season next year, because nobody celebrates the holidays like Taos (see page 98).
- Attend a film festival like the Taos Shortz Film Fest (taosshortz. com/2016/; takes place in March), or the Taos Environmental Film Festival (taosenvironmentalfilmfestival.com/; takes place in April).
- Go to the art galleries or the Taos Artists Collective, visit an artist, and buy some art.
- Take a pottery or cooking class.
- Investigate Lama (lamafoundation.org), a local spiritual place known internationally as a place of positive influence.

18

VISIT THE TAOS PUEBLO

120 Veterans Highway, Taos, NM 87571
(575) 758-1028
The pueblo lies only 3 miles from the north end of town and deserves a visit. From Taos, head north on Paseo del Norte (US 64). Stay right at the convenience store on the road called Highway to the Town of Taos.

Taos's history reaches deep into our country's past, long before written records could tell the tales. One segue from then to now is the present-day Taos Pueblo. It's the only living Native American community that holds the acclaim of being a UNESCO World Heritage Site as well as being a National Historic Landmark. This sacred dwelling is the oldest, continuously inhabited community in the nation with the main constructs likely built between the years 1000 and 1450.

The pueblo occupies 99,000 acres at 7,200 feet elevation. The pueblo inhabitants welcome visitors most days of the year except during special tribal days and from late winter to early spring. The fee, as of this writing, is under twenty dollars, but bring extra cash to purchase handmade wares from the shops and from individuals selling goods outside. You're welcome to bring a camera, but be respectful and don't invade the privacy of those living and working here by photographing them, unless you have specific permission.

The most photographed and impressive structure is what's referred to as the "apartment house" of five stories, which has been occupied since around 1450. The Taos Pueblo buildings are made of adobe, a mix of earth with water and straw. Walls are thick and the roofs are made of packed dirt. Today there are doorways, but in early times inhabitants used ladders to access openings on top. Very little else has changed here, so visiting the Taos Pueblo is like walking back in time.

Top: The Taos Pueblo, a National Historic Landmark and World Heritage Site by UNESCO. Bottom left: the river is Taos Pueblo's source for drinking water. Bottom right, from top to bottom: San Geronimo Chapel; skyline view at the Taos Pueblo.

What You Should Know about Taos Pueblo

With special events and traditions observed at the pueblo, please be respectful and follow these courtesies.

- Do not photograph tribal members without permission.
- Do not take photographs at feast days.
- Unless clearly marked as curio or store, do not enter doors.
- Do not walk in the river.
- Do not enter the adobe walls surrounding the cemetery and old church ruins.
- Do not take photographs within San Geronimo Church.

This historic site was visited by Captain Alvarado of Coronado's expedition in 1540, and he noted how well this cultured group was organized in terms of their government and irrigation systems. It's likely that these early Spanish explorers thought they had found one of the legendary cities of gold. Some say the mica in the soil gave the adobe walls the glistening effect of the precious metal. Even the unpainted pottery created from the mica-filled soil of the surrounding Sangre de Cristo Mountains has a golden-like sheen.

Go see the Taos Pueblo for yourself and get a glimpse into the ancient traditions. Tour alone or follow along with a guide (tours begin at 9:00 a.m. and run every twenty minutes on the hour). Check the Pueblo's calendar at taospueblo.com/events/ for closures and for special events like the San Geronimo Feast Day held at the end of September, the events of Christmas Eve and Christmas Day, and their July Taos Pueblo Powwow. Note: When watching ceremonial dances do not applaud afterwards, because these are not performances. Investigate the meaning ahead of time and don't be tempted to talk and ask questions during these special events.

WIN BIG AT
TAOS MOUNTAIN CASINO

19

700 Veterans Hwy, Taos, NM 87571

(575) 737-0777

The Taos Mountain Casino is located on the Taos Pueblo.
From the Taos Plaza, take Paseo Del Pueblo Norte (US 64)
to the north end of Taos. Stay right at the Allsup's–Phillips
66 Convenience Store and Service Station and proceed
north approximately 1 mile to the casino.

The Taos Mountain Casino offers hundreds of Hot Slot Machines, including penny, nickel, quarter, dollar, and five-dollar slots, for you to play. You could also try your hand at poker and keno at the video slots. The casino is non-smoking, cozy, and calls itself the Biggest Small Casino in New Mexico.

The Taos Mountain Casino is at the north end of town.

20 TOUR THE MILLICENT ROGERS MUSEUM

1504 Millicent Rogers Road, El Prado, NM 87529
(575) 758-2462
For an impressive view of Southwest history and
heritage, visit the Millicent Rogers Museum, about
ten minutes north of the Taos Plaza on NM 522/US 64.

Visitors will find over seven thousand pieces of impressive Southwest
art from jewelry to paintings and pottery. Millicent Rogers was an
heiress to the Standard Oil Company and was known as a socialite,
fashion icon, and art collector. Thankfully she ended up settling in
Taos and investing into the Taos art colony. She personally purchased
over two thousand Native American artifacts and encouraged the US
government to protect Native American art. The museum, set up in her
name by her youngest son, showcases Millicent's passion for Southwest
culture. Housed in a 1920s adobe, a hacienda with beautiful views,

Provoking art outside the Millicent Rogers Museum.

the museum has twenty galleries and exhibit spaces for its extensive collection. One section of the museum includes nearly one thousand pieces from Millicent Rogers's own collection of turquoise jewelry, including a necklace she bought in the 1940s for five thousand dollars.

Another section showcases Native American pottery from ancient times and the twentieth century's famous San Ildefonso Pueblo potter Maria Martinez. Other collections include intricate Native American baskets from the Southwest's basket-maker tribes and an impressive Hispanic religious collection. The Millicent Rogers Museum is a special place to learn about Southwest history and heritage. Take a guided tour of the museum or explore on your own, but be sure to peruse the gift shop for unique and antique items. Also, check their monthly calendar at millicentrogers.org/index.php/calendar-news for special events offered throughout the year.

SIDE TRIP: **RELAX AT OJO CALIENTE MINERAL SPRINGS SPA**

21

50 Los Banos Drive, Ojo Caliente, NM 87549
(800) 222-9162 or (505) 583-2233
Travel north on NM 522/US 64 to the Old Blinking Light
(see page 127), then turn left (west) on US 64.
Turn left (south) at County Road 115 until you reach NM 567.
Turn right (west) on NM 567 and follow the road
until you reach US 285. Turn left (south) on US 285,
then you'll pick up NM 414 west into Ojo Caliente.

Restore your mind, body, and soul at Ojo Caliente's legendary healing waters. Heated from deep within the earth and full of minerals, these natural hot springs have been soothing all sorts of folks for hundreds and hundreds of years. Native Americans were the first to utilize these hot healing waters and consider them as sacred. Rival tribes even agreed to come here in peace.

Developed commercially in the 1860s, Ojo Caliente is one of the oldest natural health spas in the country. Besides their heated pools of

Views at Ojo Caliente while soaking in the pools. (Photo credit: Chandra Perkins.)

rejuvenating waters, another pool has a special blend of mineral clay for a toxin-releasing mud bath.

The scenery surrounding these mineral baths is stunning, especially at sunset. The resort offers up all kinds of spa services (plus lodging and dining) and has 1,100 acres of trails for hiking and biking. This is a great place to get pampered, relax, and de-stress.

MARVEL AT THE RIO GRANDE GORGE BRIDGE (HIGH BRIDGE)

22

At the Old Blinking Light (see page 127), turn left (north) onto US 64/NM 522 and follow the highway for approximately 3.5 miles to the traffic signal at the intersection where if you turned east, you'd go to Arroyo Seco and Taos Ski Valley. You want to turn left to go to the bridge. Turn left (west) to continue on US 64 and travel about 8 miles. Cross the bridge (it's bouncy) and turn into the dirt parking area on the left.

The Rio Grande Gorge Bridge is one of the most-visited spots in the region and for good reason. Known locally known as the "High Bridge," this marvel is a steel deck arch bridge across the Rio Grande Gorge 12 miles northwest of Taos. You drive out from Taos westerly across wide flat land, and wham!—you come to a great deep rift in the earth. Hence the bridge.

You'll read elsewhere that the bridge is anywhere from 600 to 700 feet high, but it's 565 feet above the Rio Grande. It's listed as anywhere from the fifth to the seventh highest bridge in America. We've often joked about what the first settlers crossing in a covered wagon thought when getting to this rift and seeing no way to cross it for miles either way. "Well, Marge, this looks like a great spot to set up our cabin."

The bridge is a three-span steel (get ready for a mouthful) continuous-deck-truss structure with a concrete-filled steel-grid deck. The span is 1,280 feet: two 300-foot-long approach spans with a 600-foot-long main center span. The bridge was dedicated on September 10, 1965 and is a part of US 64, a major east–west road. You can find parking areas on both sides of the bridge. On the west side, there are local vendors hawking their wares.

The rift has been cut by eons of the Rio Grande flowing through volcanic rock, or basalt. This basalt erupted and flowed two to five million years ago. The Rio Grande originates in Southern Colorado and flows 1,900 miles from these headwaters through Colorado,

A dramatic view at the Rio Grande Gorge Bridge.

New Mexico, and Texas, and into the Gulf of Mexico.

In 1966 the American Institute of Steel Construction awarded the bridge "Most Beautiful Steel Bridge" in the "Long Span" category. The bridge has appeared in several films, including *Natural Born Killers, Twins, She's Having a Baby, Wild Hogs, Terminator Salvation,* and many others.

The bridge has cantilever platforms jutting out from the road that folks can stand out on. If you hate heights, it can be nerve-wracking and stomach-churning being out in space like that. The bridge vibrates under your feet to add to the scare factor. You're so high that the mighty Rio Grande is just a ribbon of water—sometimes tan, sometimes blue, always rocky and choppy. In summer, you can often see whitewater rafts moving slowly below.

One sad ongoing problem with the bridge is that many people commit suicide from the heights, as many as three deaths per year. At every lookout point you will see signs and emergency phones that are answered twenty-four hours a day by the New Mexico Crisis Access Hotline.

The view straight down into the gorge is grand, dramatic, even otherworldly. To the east rise the peaks of the Sangre de Cristo Mountain Range. On the west side of the bridge is the rest area where you find restrooms, parking, picnic tables, and the trailhead for the 9-mile one-way West Rim Trail (see page 78). The West Rim Trail is a moderate hike that is ideal for biking or easy walking and can also be accessed at the north end of the Orilla Verde Recreation Area.

If you want to visit the Orilla Verde Recreation Area (see page 81) and Taos Valley Overlook (see page 77) from the Gorge Bridge, turn south after you've crossed the bridge on West Rim/Upper Rim Road (Road 115), still heading south. The road ends after a few miles and you take NM 567 to Taos Junction Bridge. Cross the bridge and continue on NM 570 south.

The best photo opportunities at the High Bridge are in the morning or late afternoon, when your pics will have golden light bouncing off the basalt rocks or dramatic shadows that reveal the canyon's rugged beauty.

Old Blinking Light Intersection

The Old Blinking Light is where Taos meets the Enchanted Circle, where you can head in four directions to get to four special locales. Locals still refer to this intersection with nostalgia. At the light, you can go north on NM 522 to reach Questa; east on NM 150 to Arroyo Seco and Taos Ski Valley; and west on US 64 to Rio Grande Gorge Bridge and Earthships. As you leave Taos going north, you were on NM 522/ US 64. At the light, US 64 heads west and NM 522 goes north.

If you're caught at the light heading north, look northwest, and you can see San Antonio Peak (10,908 feet) on the horizon. It's the mountain that is softly rounded at its peak.

23 WHITEWATER RIVER RAFT DOWN THE RIO GRANDE

If you're an adventure seeker, you have to take a whitewater river rafting trip down the Rio Grande Gorge. This is world-class whitewater rafting, available year-round, with exciting class 3 and 4 rapids, but if you want a slower, less-hairy trip, all the local outfitters offer a variety of trips for every skill level.

You might want a more relaxing ride, with just a few class 2 rapids, a trip designed more for the scenery of the dramatic, volcanic rock canyon walls in the Rio Grande Gorge, natural hot springs entering the river, ancient Indian art on rocks, and all kinds of wildlife. Many outfitters even offer relaxing dinner floats.

But boy howdy, if you want to tackle the rough rapids for a challenging and wild trip, they can hook you up. The granddaddy of the trips, one of the finest in America, is the full-day Taos Box raft trip: 18 miles of intense rapids pulsing and roaring through the most awe-inspiring stretch of the Rio Grande Gorge. The outfitters need a minimum streamflow in order to raft the big rapids of the Taos Box. Because the water level is unpredictable, the availability of that trip can change at very short notice, so they could have to switch your trip to another section. Not their fault. The Taos Box is a remote chasm of steep, rugged basalt cliffs 800 feet down to the Rio Grande, loaded with sixty rapids, thirteen of which are rated class 3 and above.

Most of the raft companies serve a light lunch and water and take you by bus or have parking available for you. They will customize a tour. In summer, you'll find they offer trips twice a day: early, and right after lunch. The outfitters provide all rafting and safety equipment including life jackets and helmets, waterproof jackets and pants, and wetsuits if required. On warmer days, they'll let you jump and enjoy a quick swim in the milder stretches. Minimum age on this trip is four under most conditions. Inflatable kayaks and tubes are available to rent at several places.

Vacationing Texas family rafts the Rio Grande. (Photo credit: Mark Domme.)

Make sure you don't bring along anything that could fall out and be lost in the river. Waterproof your phone if it's not already, or get a waterproof case or use a Ziploc baggie. Wear sandals, water shoes, or old tennis or canvas shoes that can get wet. Bring a towel in your car and a change of clothes because it can get cold. The season can start as early as March and is usually best in May and June. The Taos Box can be too low to run by mid-July, but not always.

You will usually be in a paddle boat-raft where you are an integral part of powering and maneuvering the raft. Or you can request an oar boat where the guide is in full control and you can choose to paddle or just hang on. They prefer you know how to swim for self-evident reasons. You might fall out of the boat because these are intense rapids, but honestly it doesn't happen nearly as often as you might think. The guides are safety-conscious and know the river well; they won't do anything to put you in danger. They generally won't cancel trips because of rain. Rain doesn't last long in northern New Mexico and you're gonna get wet anyway.

24 SEE EARTHSHIPS AT THE EARTHSHIP BIOTECTURE WORLD HEADQUARTERS AND VISITOR CENTER

2 Earthship Way, Tres Piedras, NM 87577
(575) 613-4409

Drive west of bridge to reach this unusual mesa community and learn more at the Earthship Biotecture World Headquarters and Visitor Center. Tours are available. From Taos, north on US 64/NM 522, turn right at the light on NM 150 and turn into the parking area when you see the Earthship Biotecture sign.

So what is an Earthship? Earthships are efficient, low-carbon-footprint, off-the-grid, solar-powered homes built with natural and upcycled materials. You can find Earthships all over the world, in Europe and Africa. They appear otherworldly, indeed; in fact, spaceship-y, sort of Buck Rogers meets steampunk meets hippie. You'll get the sense that the out-of-this-world community was once a movie set for a sci-fi flick.

The Earthship architecture concept was formulated in the 1970s by architect Michael Reynolds who wanted create homes that would be able to do three things: 1) utilize sustainable architecture and materials indigenous to the local area or recycled materials wherever possible; 2) rely on natural energy sources and be independent from the grid; and

---

Six Principles of Earthships

An Earthship addresses the following needs:

- Thermal and solar heating and cooling
- Solar and wind electricity
- Protected and contained sewage treatment
- Building with natural and recycled materials
- Water harvesting of rain and snow
- Sustainable organic food production

The creatively designed and sustainable Earthship homes north of Taos.

3) be reasonable for a person with no specialized construction skills to build. So basically, these houses are off-grid, earth-bermed, passive solar homes with exterior walls made of old tires packed with dirt.

SOAK IN THE MANBY AND BLACK ROCK HOT SPRINGS 25

Not often do you find natural hot springs in such accessible locations and with such accompanying wildness and beauty. Here are two such hot springs.

MANBY HOT SPRINGS

Five miles from NM 522 (north of Taos), turn west on County Road B007. Drive about 2.5 miles on County Road B007 then turn left onto a dirt road. This road can be rough with ruts and washboards, so high-clearance

The welcoming waters to soak in at Black Rock Hot Springs.

vehicles are recommended (might be easier on a mountain bike). You will see the Dobson House sign, then turn left at the next fork. Stay right and you'll finally reach the parking area. The path to the springs is to the left of the parking area.

Manby Hot Springs is a beautiful natural hot springs on the Rio Grande River. These magma-heated pools have been enticing soakers since the Native Americans discovered these warm waters deep in the gorge. Look closely, as there are a couple of petroglyphs to prove their presence. Spaniards and stagecoach entrepreneurs spent time here too. In fact, these springs are sometimes referred to as Stagecoach Springs. In the early 1900s, Arthur Manby had his own plans for these pools and built a bathhouse over one of them. Some say his ghost still roams the area trying to find a little peace in these mineral waters.

The hike from the parking area isn't too bad (classified as moderate, being fifteen to thirty minutes) but is a little rocky with a steady decline and some drop-off edges that may not make it suitable for little ones. That said, we see children at the springs. Overall, the hike should take about fifteen to thirty minutes one way. After soaking, the inclined hike back up may not be as easy as the hike down, so bring good sturdy shoes to help you along. Remember that these are primitive pools with no services; it's all nature out here, including a few clothing-optional soakers you could encounter. For the most part, depending on the season and time of day, you might have the springs all to yourself or you might be sharing it with a few folks. The larger pool seems to be the warmest and can squeeze in ten or so people. The smaller pools, closer to the river's edge, are sometimes covered by river water when it's running high. Overall, the temperature of the pools ranges from around ninety-four to one hundred degrees Fahrenheit. Come sit and soak in these age-old heated pools. Gaze at the high cliffs above. Feel the minerals and beauty of the land restore your soul.

BLACK ROCK HOT SPRINGS

Drive across the John Dunn Bridge over the Rio Grande (B007) and turn left going uphill a bit. You'll find a small parking area at the first switchback with enough room for only a few cars.

The trail is classified as easy but does have a few rocky sections and a few narrow spots on the edge. The hike down is about a quarter of a mile and doesn't take too long. Take your time, keep your footing. If you aren't a strong hiker, use a pole or walking stick.

Black Rock Hot Springs is another primitive spring filled with warm, relaxing waters heated from hot magma below. It's relatively small, with the main pool about 12 feet around. Black Rock sits on the west side of the Rio Grande in the gorge. The lower pool is easily covered by river water during runoff season (May and early June), and when the river gets a little high, cold water flows in. On average, the larger pool's temperature stays at about ninety-seven degrees Fahrenheit. The bottoms of the pools are muddy and the interior rocks can be slick. There are plenty of rocks around the edge if you prefer to sit with your feet in instead of fully immersing. Since Black Rock Hot Springs is so easy to get to, it's popular and often crowded. But last time we were there, we had it all to ourselves. It was quiet and perfect and, of course, beautiful as always. Again, remember that you may come across soakers who are au natural.

26

SIDE TRIP:
EXPLORE ARROYO SECO

Seco Village Association, 480 SR 150,
Arroyo Seco, NM 87514
(575) 776-5183

As you drive up NM 150 from Taos, the road meanders back and forth and all of a sudden, 3 miles up, the road slows and narrows, so slow down because the speed limit lowers considerably, and then bam!—you're in Arroyo Seco, halfway up to Taos Ski Valley.

Arroyo Seco is a charming spot in the road between Taos and the Taos Ski Valley, and is definitely worth exploring. This unincorporated village is quaint, laid-back, and full of art, shops, restaurants, a famous ice cream shop (Taos Cow), and lots of charisma. Park your car in one of the parking lots and get out and walk to get the full effect of this mountain community. Buy locally made art, trinkets, antiques, and some of the best handmade ice cream around.

Lots of stars are rumored to live in this artist's community

Arroyo Seco's main street exudes the town's quirky, cool vibe.

located right at the foot of towering Taos Mountain. Arroyo Seco means "dry stream" in Spanish, but water still runs in the small creek behind some of the storefronts. A couple of notable photo ops include the flying pig on top of one of the shops and the 1950 Chevy pickup parked in the small parking lot by the mercantile.

The Church of the Most Holy Trinity was completed in 1834 and has recently been restored. Arroyo Seco, often referred to as Seco, was settled in 1804 on a Spanish land grant. Local history includes the Martinez brothers who planted crops and built the first houses here as well as folklore about the appearance of a holy image. The folklore says that the valley was dedicated to the Most Holy Trinity since the image was found here and the Trinity had chosen the valley as its home. Today, this holy image is kept in Arroyo Seco's historic Catholic church, which was completed in 1834.

At 10,780 feet, Lucero Peak overlooks Arroyo Seco and houses a cave that the Taos Pueblo population finds sacred. D.H. Lawrence visited this historic cave back in 1924 and it's said to be the inspiration for his short story "The Woman Who Rode Away." Lots of people have visited Arroyo Seco since that time and many have called Seco their home, including an array of folks from hippies and Gen Xers to actors and politicians and all kind of souls in between. Some days you may

Looking for Something Different to Do in Arroyo Seco?

- Attend a hot yoga class at Hot Yoga Taos (482A NM 150, Arroyo Seco, NM 87514).
- Visit one of Seco's restaurants and get ice cream from Taos Cow (485 NM 150, Arroyo Seco, NM 87514).
- Attend a free Seco Live music event. Visit secolive.org for upcoming events.
- Celebrate at the Christmas party with Santa, cookies, and cider (find details at visitseco.com/)

only see a few people sauntering along the main street, but on special event days, like the Fourth of July, the place is packed for a day of fun. In fact, the Fourth of July parade is somewhat famous; it's quirky, varied, and only a block long. Seco has an historic, hippie-like comfort that gives visitors a sense of tranquility and a taste of New Mexico's past.

27 FISH THE RIO HONDO

We had to highlight these favorite fishing spots on the Enchanted Circle, but you could find more on page 33.

UPPER RIO HONDO

This little gem follows alongside NM 522 on your way from above Arroyo Seco all the way up to Taos Ski Valley. There are lots of pullouts along the way. Be careful walking on the side of road. The occasional bear meanders along the banks, so heads up. Small wild

Angler fishing the confluence of the Lower Hondo and the Rio Grande.

browns thrive here. If you can get over being so close to the road, get over the noise of occasional traffic, it's a gorgeous little stream in beautiful forest.

LOWER RIO HONDO

A little tricky to reach, but if you want to see the John Dunn Bridge then it's worth the effort. There are big pools connected by long runs and pocket water, undercut banks, big boulders. It fishes well in fall and winter (spring-fed, so it's warmer) when the trout from Rio Grande run up the stream. The road (B007) runs right beside the river so just pull over in any number of pullouts and hop in a pool.

SIDE TRIP: **SKI AND SNOWBOARD AT TAOS SKI VALLEY** 28

116 Sutton Place, Taos Ski Valley, NM 87525
(800) 776-1111

From Arroyo Seco on NM 150 and across a high plain, see the community of Arroyo Hondo in the valley below before you turn northerly into the canyon. Look to your right for the Upper Rio Hondo, a clear cold creek. The road winds back and forth and traffic often stacks up, so if you don't like vehicles on your tail, you might pull over at one of the numerous pullouts. Keep an eye out for wildlife as you drive, especially early and late in the day. The speed limit drops to 15 miles per hour as you enter Taos Ski Valley city limits.

Taos Ski Valley is one of the unsung ski communities in the West, an undiscovered gem where the

The slopes at Taos Ski Valley, known for its world-class skiing.

Southwest meets Europe, pueblo meets chalet. A former miner's camp, Taos Ski Valley (TSV) is long a favorite of seasoned skiers since the terrain reminds one so much of steep, challenging downhill skiing of the Alps. "Steep and deep" has been a motto associated with these slopes since its inception. Taos Ski Valley was built from Ernie Blake's vision in 1954 as a chalet-style architectural homage to ski villages in Europe.

The ski town is casual, slow-living with less than one hundred people residing there year-round. For sixty years Taos Ski Valley has been relatively undeveloped, but that is changing—good news for some, dreaded for others. We believe that with the proposed changes and increased development, Taos Ski Valley will move into the twenty-first century while maintaining much of its 1960s feel and down-to-earth ambience. We've spent a good amount of time at the resort's new slopeside Blake Hotel. Opened in 2017, the gorgeous hotel includes an exquisite art collection and decor, sophisticated rooms, an inspired spa, and attentive customer service. Even the walls of the halls are fun and informational.

Taos Ski Valley Stats

Average annual snowfall: 305 inches

Average days of sunshine: 300+ days

Base elevation: 9,200 feet

Summit elevation: 12,481 feet

Vertical drop: 3,281 feet

Number of trails: 110 total: 24% beginner, 25% intermediate, 51% expert

Number of lifts: 15 total: 4 quads, 3 triples, 5 doubles, 3 surface lifts

Hours of lift operation: 9:00 a.m.–4:00 p.m.

Uphill capacity: more than 15,000 skiers per hour

Snowmaking capabilities: 100% of beginner and intermediate slopes

Total acreage: 1,294 acres

—from Taos Ski Valley, skitaos.com/discover-taos/history/

WINTER in Taos Ski Valley

Taos Ski Valley has maintained its charm and old-school feel even with the change of ownership and upgrades. Thank goodness. The family feel that Ernie Blake, founder and longtime owner, established is what draws lots of people to this mountain. That and of course its three hundred-plus days of sunshine, three hundred-plus inches of snow each year, and its killer slopes over twelve-hundred-some odd acres don't hurt either. Taos Ski Valley is a small incorporated village with fewer than one hundred people in permanent residence. But there's plenty of lodging, restaurants, and shopping for visitors in this European-styled atmosphere.

Skiers (and snowboarders since 2008) flock to this world-class mountain in the snowy months. Taos is known around the globe, especially for its extreme and advanced skiing options. In fact, when you first look at the mountain it can be a little overwhelming to a newbie or good old intermediate skier who skis every few years or so. There's even a sign at the base reassuring worriers that there are plenty of skiable runs for everyone, even beginners.

With the new ownership there are new runs, improved snowmaking, a new chair lift to the advanced Kachina Peak (12,451 feet), an updated Children's Center, and a gondolita to help the littles, and parents, easily traverse from the Children's Center to the Resort Plaza by the Blake Hotel.

As far as ski schools go, Taos has one of the best reputations around. The Ernie Blake Snowsports School has loads of options for kids, teens, and adults, whether you're just starting out or wanting to hone your skills. They are proud to say that you'll leave here a better skier than when you started. Be sure to get reservations ahead of time by calling (575) 776-2291.

Other wintertime options off the ski mountain are plentiful at Ski Valley. You're near beautiful trails for snowshoeing, like the 4-mile round-trip Williams Lake Trail. The lake will likely be frozen and you just may catch a friendly game of hockey. Go at this snowshoe hike yourself, or take a guided tour like the peaceful full-moon snowshoe hike (call (800) 758-5262 for more information). Backcountry and cross-country skiers have plenty of trail options too. Snowmobiling is also popular in the Valley. You can rent and zoom around on a guided trip up to 12,000 feet in elevation (call (575) 751-6051 for reservations), or if you have your own snowmobile, then you have lots of national forest options that aren't too far away. For a family-friendly option right on the mountain, you can get in lots of fun zipping down the tubing hill starting at 5:00 p.m., with rentals available. As for sledding, a popular spot off the mountain and on the other side of Taos is US Hill, about ten minutes or so from Taos off Upper Ranchitos Road, right in the Carson National Forest. Of course, the après-ski options at TSV are easily accessible at the base, whether you're sitting outside and watching the action or cozied up inside. The après-ski scene has improved, and so have the eating options. Shop in the European village for ski stuff, souvenirs and trinkets, outfitting gear, or all kinds of other things unique to TSV and northern New Mexico.

Keep an eye on TSV's yearly calendar of events at skitaos.com/events-calendar/. There are several races and competitions on the mountain for skiers and boarders. Check with mountain officials for the details.

TSV also has a Military Mondays program where many Mondays are set aside for military personnel, active or retired, to receive special discounts on lift tickets and lodging. Immediate family is included. Be sure to call ahead for details on dates and discounts.

SUMMER in Taos Ski Valley

Summer in the Taos Ski Valley brings cool temperatures and a colorful backdrop of flowers and foliage. Ride chairlift number 4 up for breathtaking views of Kachina and Wheeler Peaks then hike down from 12,000 feet. The hike usually takes about an hour, depending on how long you like to stop for photo ops or just to soak in the beauty and mountain views. The top is a great place for a picnic, so consider packing some easy-

Looking for Something Different to Do in Taos Ski Valley?

- Sit by the fire pit at the base and watch the skiers.
- Sip on a Mocha Maya or another warm drink.
- Hang out at Tim's Stray Dog Cantina and have a bowl of pork green-chile stew.
- Rock climb with a guide or take a horseback riding trip (taosskivalley.com/play/summer-activities/).
- Sip wine and eat a gourmet flatbread at 192 at the Blake, a restaurant centered around a communal fireplace at the Blake Hotel.
- Shop for cool mountain gear or a souvenir T-shirt.

to-carry treats. You can always ride the lift back down if that suits your needs. There are plenty of trails around the ski area that warrant a hike, including the hike to Williams Lake and Wheeler Peak (the highest point in New Mexico; see page 142).

Other active summer adventures like mountain biking at the challenging Northside terrain or rock climbing, horseback riding, and fishing the Rio Hondo give outdoor enthusiasts plenty to do in the ski valley. There are also numerous fishing options near TSV (see page 33 for more information).

When you're ready to wind down, relax with some of the outdoor music performances or attend an educational program. The Taos Ski Valley calendar at taosskivalley.com/events has all the latest information for performances and programs. Fourth of July is a festive time with live music at the Bavarian, a rubber duck race, chairlift rides, beer, and brats. Later on, August brings about a popular 10K trail run.

Overall, summer in Taos Ski Valley is calm, quiet, and not crowded. The air is cool and relaxing, with aspen leaves lightly quaking in the breeze and the Rio Hondo gently flowing like musical notes over the creek bed. Temperatures in Taos are usually ten to fifteen degrees warmer, which, in summer, means TSV is perfection.

HIKE TO WILLIAMS LAKE

29

Distance: 5 miles round-trip
Elevation gain: 1,500 feet
Trailhead: Go through all the ski parking lots, and stay left.
Turn right on Twining Road, left on Phoenix Road,
and park in the hiker's parking lot. Here is where the
other hikes in Taos Ski Valley area begin as well.

This hike is probably the most popular of all the hikes in the
Enchanted Circle. The elevation gain is only 1,500 feet and it takes
place in the Questa Ranger District/Wheeler Peak Wilderness from
the Taos Ski Valley upper parking lot. From the lot, hike immediately
uphill on the east side of a ski run alongside Lake Fork Creek, a cute
bubbly little stream.

You'll segue onto an old road, Trail 62. We've seen people of
all ages hike this trail, but you'll want to stop from time to time to
catch your breath. When you crest the last hill, Williams Lake lies in
front of you with Wheeler Peak rising behind it. Make sure to visit

*The well-traveled alpine lake hike is perfect for four-legged friends and
people of all ages.*

the waterfall on the other side of the lake. If you stay at the bottom, it's not as impressive as when you scramble up the rocks and see the waterfall above.

You are at 11,000-feet elevation. There are no fish in this lake—it's too shallow and freezes solid in winter. You might sometimes catch folks playing ice hockey here in winter. Some take group moonlight hikes to the lake in summer. Unless the snow is deep, folks hike up to the lake year-round. All around you are spruce, rock fields, meadows, wildflowers, waterfall. Often you'll see hikers with dogs or runners flitting like elves atop the rocky trail.

Other Hikes around Taos Ski Valley

WHEELER PEAK TRAIL 90

Distance: 14 miles round-trip

Elevation gain: 3,761 feet

Trailhead: The trail begins at Twining Campground.

The hike to Wheeler Peak (13,161 feet) is one of the finest, most dramatic, most breathtaking in the Southwest. This is the highest mountain in New Mexico and from the summit you can view the state's tallest mountains, some of the peaks in Colorado, the Rio Grande Gorge, the only alpine tundra mat in the state, pika and marmot, and so much more that make this hike memorable.

From Twining Campground, the trail heads uphill at Long Canyon Creek toward Bull of the Woods Pasture. You'll cross Long Canyon Creek and reach the pasture at about 2.25 miles. Stay on the road that goes up to Bull of the Woods Mountain. From there the trail is defined and above timberline.

WILLIAMS LAKE TRAIL 62/WHEELER PEAK SUMMIT TRAIL 67

Distance: 8 miles round-trip

Elevation gain: 2,961 feet

Trailhead: Two miles on the way to Williams Lake, you will come to the junction with Trail 67, the Wheeler Peak Trail. The Wheeler Peak Trail is to your left at the junction.

After only a half-mile of climbing Trail 67, you will emerge from the tree line. It's breathtaking, the sweeping vistas, the wildness and ruggedness, and the majestic bigness of it all.

The trail ascends at a consistent grade, so you can move without having to stop a lot. The trail paths are clear and easy to follow.

What You Should Know about Wheeler Peak Trail

- The summit gets crowded on weekends, so plan accordingly.
- Beginners can do this hike, but it's a long one. The ascent alone takes three to five hours.
- Spend a few days at altitude before you hike or you could end up nauseated and have a bad headache from altitude sickness.
- The weather can change quickly at any time and that means rain, cold, snow, sleet, wind, sun, and heat. Take a jacket and layer so you can put up with getting hot and chilly.
- During the monsoon season (July and August), watch the forecast. You should start early and get off the ridgeline early. You don't want to be exposed on the mountain if afternoon thunderstorms roll in.
- Wear sunblock, because you are closer to the sun and its UV rays. You also don't have trees or shade for much of the hike.

TRAVEL TO THE JOHN DUNN BRIDGE

30

To reach John Dunn Bridge from Taos Ski Valley, turn right (north) on NM 522 where you'll continue past the cutoff for the Taos Pueblo and enter into the valley highlighted by views of Taos Mountain to the east and volcanic cones out west. Cross the Rio Hondo and then take a left on the road directly after mile marker 6 to access the bridge. From Taos, follow NM 522 north to B007 to reach the bridge.

One of the central locations for outdoor activities and sightseeing is at and near the John Dunn Bridge in Arroyo Hondo. This impressive bridge crosses the Rio Grande near where the Rio Hondo enters the big river. This area sees lots of traffic because this is one of the only drivable access points to the river—one of only three crossings over the river in the national monument—but also because people like to come here for whitewater rafting, fishing, kayaking, swimming, soaking, climbing, and picnicking.

The bridge was built

The John Dunn Bridge marks a popular recreational spot along the Rio Grande River.

in 1908 by namesake John Dunn. Dunn hauled travelers and mail all over the area and into Taos. Dunn was into everything; he ran a stagecoach, delivered mail, and operated a hotel, bar, restaurant, and gambling parlor on the site. Almost none of this remains today. The bridge was washed out and then later replaced, so this is the third one at this location, built in 1930. You can find several Native American petroglyphs on the cliff facing along the Rio Grande. Watch for hot air balloons that float over the bridge and down the canyon.

This recreation area is also the main launch point for rafters and kayakers who fight strong waters that run between 650- to 800-foot basalt walls. They travel through the 17-mile stretch of the river known as the Taos Box. Whitewater rafting through Taos Box has sixty rapids, some of the most famous whitewater rapids in the world. Thirteen of those are rated class 3 and above. The river also has several class 4+ and 5 rapids when the water is high. At Taos Junction Bridge the river becomes calm.

Taos has several reliable rafting outfitters who can put you on the kind of water you can actually handle. The whitewater rafting rushes through a chasm in a wilderness declared by Congress as one of the nation's first Wild and Scenic Rivers. You have a great chance at seeing the gorge's wildlife inhabitants: bighorn sheep, river otters, elk, beavers, mountain lions, ravens, falcons, and eagles.

Five climbing walls lie in the John Dunn area with skill levels for all. You can also take a short hike back down to the Black Rock Hot Springs (see page 133).

VISIT THE D.H. LAWRENCE RANCH

506 D.H. Lawrence Ranch Road, Taos, NM 87564
(505) 277-5572
Come visit for free this 160-acre enclave, just 20 miles north
of Taos, open Thursdays, Fridays, and Saturdays.
From John Dunn Bridge, take NM 522 north. Drive up a dirt
road (D.H. Lawrence Road) to reach the destination.
Signs will lead the way along the road.

31

It may be surprising to some that British author D.H. Lawrence was memorialized right here in New Mexico. Even though he only resided in the Taos area for eleven months over the course of a few years, what's now known as the D.H. Lawrence Ranch was the only piece of property he and his wife ever owned. Lawrence once said that being in

New Mexico was "the greatest experience we ever had from the outside world. It certainly changed me forever." Lawrence, like so many other writers and creative types, was drawn to Taos and its surrounds.

This famed writer of works like *Lady Chatterley's Lover* was sought out by socialite and patron of the arts Mabel Dodge (Sterne) Luhan to come to Taos. Mabel kept company with a litany of interesting folks, including Georgia O'Keeffe and Ansel Adams. Intrigued, Lawrence and his wife, Frieda, headed to Taos in the fall of 1922. The Lawrences continued their travels, but Lawrence, not

The Lawrence memorial at the D.H. Lawrence Ranch.

The famous Lawrence Tree, and the view of it that Georgia O'Keeffe painted.

able to give up Taos, tried to convince friends to join him in returning to this Southwest enclave.

Artist Dorothy Brett took the Lawrences up on the invitation and the three headed to Taos. Mabel Luhan ended up offering her Kiowa Ranch to Lawrence and Frieda. Some say she wanted to keep Lawrence in Taos, so she made him the generous offer of her 160-acre ranch. He turned down the gift, but Frieda offered up one of his manuscripts as payment. And so, the D.H. Lawrence Ranch history began.

Even though the living conditions at the ranch were a little rough, the beauty of the land and the enchantment of the Taos area made up for any deficiencies in lodging. Inspired by the land, Lawrence finished writing his short novel, *St. Mawr*, in which readers can sense his fondness for the ranch's landscape. The Lawrences' and Lady Brett's cabins are still standing on the ranch for visitors to see and for Lawrence aficionados to connect with the writer's influences of the time.

A now famous piece of nature, the "Lawrence Tree"—a large pine tree standing outside his homestead cabin—continues to enchant visitors as it did Lawrence. He was known to write under this tall pine at a carpenter's table, noting "the green top no one ever looks at" and equating the tree's trunk to standing like a "guardian angel." After Lawrence's death, artist Georgia O'Keeffe painted *The Lawrence Tree* from the vantage point of lying down on Lawrence's workbench and gazing up through the tree's branches.

After being diagnosed with tuberculosis in Mexico, Lawrence returned to Taos for his last time in 1925. He spent several months writing *The Plumed Serpent* and *David*, a biblical drama. He returned to Europe on his fortieth birthday that same year and always hoped to go back to Taos. Lawrence had said, "It is the ghosts one misses most, the ghosts there, of the Rocky Mountains, that never go beyond the timber. I know them, they know me: we go well together."

Lady Brett ended up making Taos her permanent home, and Frieda and Angelo Ravagli, the man who became her third husband, also returned to Taos to live on the ranch and to build a memorial for Lawrence.

Frieda later had Lawrence's body exhumed in Europe and brought his ashes to New Mexico. Some say that Lawrence's ashes are mixed with the plaster used to make his memorial stone. Apparently Lady Brett and Mabel Dodge Luhan wanted the ashes scattered across the ranch, but Frieda wanted it done her way and dumped the ashes in the mix, keeping the two ladies from his ashes. It seems that the three women had all vied for Lawrence's attention during their time together in Taos.

No matter how you interpret the story, this is the place to honor Lawrence, his life, his writings, his time in New Mexico. The property is now under ownership of the University of New Mexico, as Frieda requested in her will, and is listed on the National Register of Historic Places. This former Kiowa ranch lies at 8,600 feet in elevation and has inspired Lawrence and many others to tap into their creativity and contribute to the arts.

32 FISH THE RED RIVER FISH HATCHERY

1 State Route 515, Questa, NM 87556
(575) 586-0222
Leaving the D.H. Lawrence Ranch on NM 522,
going downhill and just before mile marker 17,
you'll come to the turnoff for the Red River
Fish Hatchery (around 22 miles from Taos Plaza).
Turn left (west) at Junction 515.

This attraction (no entrance fee) is the rearing station for the trout that stock the rivers and lakes in the northern New Mexico region. The hatchery raises over two million trout a year (three-inchers, five-inchers, ten-inchers, and fifteen-inchers), and since the fish are sterilized, their sole purpose is for anglers to try to catch them.

The facility includes a kid's fishing pond, a self-guided tour, several raceways full of trout, a small visitor center, and a large show pond full of some of the biggest trout you'll ever see. You can feed the fish if the food dispensers have food in them. Anglers can also park and fish the Red River

Loads of healthy trout ready to be stocked in waters nearby.

upstream or downstream from here. The facility stocks some nice-sized trout up and down the river near the facility.

Fishing is great for stocked trout in the pools and pocket water up and down from the hatchery. Flyfishers and spin-fishers both do well for the stocked trout. Make sure not to crowd other anglers in this small river.

Hike Pescado Trail

Distance: 3.8 miles round-trip

Elevation gain: 800 feet

Trailhead: You can park at the hatchery (22 miles from Taos) or the Wild Rivers Visitor Center (1120 Cerro Road, Cerro, NM 87519; 38 miles from Taos).

This low-trafficked trail that follows the river connects the Red River Fish Hatchery to the Wild Rivers Visitor Center. In the summer months, this is a moderately difficult hike. Many don't know you can use the trail in the winter, and if you get snow some folks will snowshoe or cross-country ski it. The trail for the first mile from the Wild River Visitor Center is flat and rocky then traverses a somewhat steep path with switchbacks, and then it descends an old mining road to the hatchery.

OTHER THINGS
to See and Do from Taos to Questa

CENTRAL VOLCANOES REGION

Starting at the Rio Grande Gorge Bridge (see directions to the Rio Grande Gorge Bridge on page 125), drive northwest on US 64 for about 3 miles to a dirt road on the right. Follow this road straight east for several miles then turn north onto BLM Road TP 130. Note that few roads are maintained, and summer rains or winter snows make for treacherous conditions. Inquire with BLM-Taos by calling (575) 758-8851 for current conditions.

The Central Volcanoes Region has a series of extinct volcanic cones that rise up from the sagebrush plateau. The cones generally date from 1.8 to 4 million years. The oldest volcanic cone is 22 million years old, around the time when the Rio Grande Rift opened. Imagine the volcano erupting, with massive flows of basalt and rhyolite lava spreading out over the plains of northern New Mexico. The largest of the imposing cones are Cerro de la Olla (9,475 feet), Cerro del Aire (9,023 feet), Cerro Montoso (8,655 feet), and Cerro Chiflo (8,976 feet).

RIO SAN ANTONIO WILDERNESS STUDY AREA, SAN ANTONIO MOUNTAIN, RIO SAN ANTONIO

Starting at the Rio Grande Gorge Bridge (see directions to the Rio Grande Gorge Bridge on page 125) drive northwest on US 64 to the village of Tres Piedras. Turn north on US 285 and drive about 15 miles. Turn west onto FR 118 north of San Antonio Mountain and drive about 3 miles to a small dirt trail that goes north along the eastern side of the little canyon. Drive north along the dirt road to reach the Wilderness Study Area. 4WDs are recommended.

This is for those of you who really need a long day trip, since the distance from Taos Plaza is about 51 miles. Set in the northwest corner of the Rio Grande del Norte National Monument, the Rio San Antonio section acts like a microcosm of the Rio Grande ecosystem and is even more remote. There are rolling grasslands and the extinct volcano known as San Antonio Mountain (10,908 feet).

The Rio San Antonio is a small fishable river that has cut through basalt layers, and the result is that it favors a tiny dioramic Rio Grande Gorge. Because everything is so flat, you wouldn't even suspect there is a gorge or a river. You won't find any designated trails even though this is one of the better angling spots in northern New Mexico.

Bring binoculars and long-lens cameras. The open terrain provides incredible visibility so you can spot wildlife including elk, mule deer, pronghorn, black bears, mountain lions, coyotes, prairie dogs, wild turkeys, raptors such as red-tailed hawks, bald eagles, and peregrine falcons. You could also go fishing, hiking, bird watching, wildlife viewing, hunting, cross-country skiing, and camping.

The Rio de los Pinos is a wild and isolated stream.

RIO DE LOS PINOS

Starting at the Rio Grande Gorge Bridge (see directions to the Rio Grande Gorge Bridge on page 125) drive northwest on US 64 to the village of Tres Piedras. Turn north on US 285 and drive about 20 miles north, just across the Colorado border. Turn west on County Road C to the village of San Antonio. Take County Road 12.5 southwest to County Road 443. Follow County Road 443, which brings you back across the state border and then into the Rios de los Pinos area.

Poised to land a rare Rio Grande cutthroat.

The Rio de los Pinos ("River of the Pines") is so far from the Enchanted Circle (more than two hours' drive) it seems unlikely that anyone would do this as a day trip, so we will be brief about this wild and gorgeous area. The Rio de los Pinos is one of my favorite fishing spots in New Mexico and Colorado, but it's so remote and wild that it's recommended you go into the area with a veteran or a guide.

The river flows from Colorado's San Juan Mountains into New Mexico through deep canyons, heavy pine forests, and several meadows until, after 20 miles, the clear cold stream runs back across the Colorado border near the village of Antonito. The Rio de los Pinos is one of the best fly-fishing rivers in New Mexico with healthy populations of both Rio Grande cutthroat, rainbow, and brown trout.

TAOS PLATEAU PRAIRIE

Distance from Taos Plaza is about 50 miles. Starting at the Rio Grande Gorge Bridge (see directions to the Rio Grande Gorge Bridge on page 125) drive northwest on US 64 to the village of Tres Piedras. Turn north on US 285 and drive about 17 miles. Turn east onto a signed BLM Road TP 120 towards Pinabetoso Peaks and you'll see the prairie before you.

For as far as you can see, the prairie spreads to the north, a vast grassland atop the Taos Plateau volcanic field. These sheet flows of basalt and rhyolite lava make up the north central portion of the monument. This section is the second largest volcanic field in the Rio Grande Rift.

This is wild and remote country. Have water, snacks, jackets, and a spare tire aired up. The roads get yucky and mucky when wet. You'll see rolling hills of grass and sage. Pinabetoso Peaks are some of the youngest volcanic cones in the monument. Watch for cactus. Bring binoculars because you might spot wildlife including the scaled quail, mountain plover, western burrowing owl, ferruginous hawk, and a whole host of migratory birds. You may also spot Gunnison's prairie dogs, pronghorns, swift foxes, badgers, box turtles, and tarantulas. You'd be surprised by how many visitors talk about seeing tarantulas throughout the monument. The area is good for hunting and stargazing.

FROM QUESTA
TO RED RIVER

QUESTA

Route: From Taos Plaza, take US 64 north for 3 miles to NM 522;
go north on NM 522 for 20 miles to Questa.
Elevation: 7,461 feet
Population: 1,754
Lay of the land: canyons (to west and east), valley surrounded
by mountains, river

The population of Questa is about 1,750 so it's not a large town at all. Located near the confluence of the Rio Grande and the Red River, Questa is the least tourist-oriented town on the Enchanted Circle Scenic Byway and definitely not a resort town (yet). Questa sits at an elevation of 7,461 feet on the western edge of the Sangre de Cristo Mountains. In its early decades, Questa was a hot spot for traders and others on the old Taos Trail. The villagers survived regular attacks by Utes and Apaches.

Questa was officially founded in 1842, a tough and tumbling village, one of many that sprung up in northern New Mexico and southern Colorado along the Rio Grande. Questa was originally known as San Antonio del Rio Colorado ("Saint Anthony of the Red River"). The name Questa (misspelled by Anglos from the original "cuesta") means "ridge" or "hill." The Sangre de Cristo Mountains surround the village, and if you look closely you'll see a big white Q on the side of a mountain.

The village has a large Hispanic population and the economy was historically largely dependent on agriculture as well as income from a now-closed Chevron molybdenum mine. Mining was a part of Questa's heritage since the Moly Mine was opened in 1918. Molybdenum, which is used in steel alloys, was formed during volcanic activity over twenty-five million years ago. The mine sustained the local economy for generations, but in June 2014 the mine closed permanently due

Top, left to right: the Red River on its way to Questa; St. Anthony's Church.
Bottom: beautiful views on the way to Questa from Taos.

to poor market conditions. Now Questa is looking to rebrand itself around the myriad opportunities for outdoor recreation. Many residents also commute from Questa to Taos, Red River, and Angel Fire to work in the hospitality industries there.

You won't find the hotels and restaurants in Questa that you'll find in the other Enchanted Circle towns, but if you can rent a house or cabin, it's an ideal home base for winter and summer sports. Questa also has a thriving artist's community.

But we do see evidence that Questa is becoming more and more attuned to providing lodging (cabins especially), and why not? Red River runs right behind the village. Questa is centrally located: Rio Grande and Wild Rivers to the west/northwest; canyon and Red River to the east; Valle Vidal to the north; fishing and biking to the south.

Biking and fishing are popular options in the Rio Grande del Norte National Monument (see page 165). You get a 22-mile round-trip of paved road with little traffic from the park entrance or 6 miles around the scenic loop. No fewer than six trails take you from the rim into the gorge where you can fish in some of the prettiest scenery in the West. If you like hiking in summer or cross-country skiing in winter, consider the flat Rinconada Loop Trail (see page 170).

Cabresto Lake and Creek (see page 179) is popular for those who enjoy hiking, backpacking, fishing, snowshoeing, snowmobiling and OHVers. Farther east in the canyon are numerous hiking opportunities like Columbine (see page 163) and Goose Creek (see page 197). Bottom line, Questa is an ideal home base for any recreationalist.

Looking for Something Different to Do in Questa?

- Photograph the beautiful scenery.
- Stop at the National Historical Marker for La Cienega School building, opened in 1936 and built by the WPA (Works Progress Administration), just outside Questa on your way to Red River.
- Go big-game hunting in the fall.

VISIT ST. ANTHONY'S CHURCH

10 Church Plaza, Questa, NM 87556
(505) 586-0470

As you turn on NM 38 towards Red River from Questa,
you'll see a green sign for St. Anthony's Catholic Church.
Turn left at the sign and then turn right when you get up
the hill. At the top of the hill, turn left into the parking lot.

One must-visit site in Questa is St. Anthony's Church, the town's
lifeblood and community center for 170 years. The original structure
was built in 1840–41, but what you see today is the result of a massive
renovation project that took several years—a gorgeous revision of a
mid-nineteenth-century adobe church. The church has thick adobe
walls, stained glass windows, huge vigas and corbels, and high
airy ceilings. The church has massive buttresses at the back with
an adobe-walled courtyard in front. This is a great photo op from
numerous angles and times of day.

The lovingly restored St. Anthony's Church in Questa.

34 FISH EAGLE ROCK LAKE

From Questa's Main Street (NM 522), turn right (east) onto NM 38 and travel 2 miles. The lake is off to your right.

You'll see right away that this is not your typical day-use lake. First, this is some awfully gorgeous scenery with mountains all around. Second, Eagle Rock Lake and Red River are connected by trails and recent habitat improvement in an effort to improve fishing. The Eagle Rock Day Use Area now has a stream that has better holding water with tree trunks and large boulders creating pools and deeper water. Bridges and trails allow easy access for hikers and anglers. The park offers fishing for rainbow trout in both the lake and Red River behind

Eagle Rock Lake makes a nice stopping point from Questa to Red River.

it. You can hike around the lake on the improved trail or follow the river. The park is ideal for picnicking, taking a break from driving, or taking great photos of the mountain vistas. It's also a perfect spot for your kids to try their hand at fishing.

That transition recently received a boost as the New Mexico Department of Game and Fish partnered with Chevron Mining, Inc., Trout Unlimited, Questa Economic Development Board, the Bureau of Land Management, and US Forest Service on a fish habitat improvement project at Eagle Rock Lake and the Red River. The project involved installing large boulders and tree trunks as well as reconfiguring the streambed to increase pools and create better places for fish to live. Gravel bars were built to increase river channel sinuosity, and new trails and bridges were developed to improve angler access.

While improvements were being made to the river reaches,

Hike Columbine Canyon Trail #71

Distance: 4 miles, 6 miles, or 11 miles (for three different hikes)

Elevation gain: 400 feet, 2,000 feet, and 3,200 feet

Trailhead: The trailhead is at the south end of the Columbine Campground. From Red River, travel west on NM 38 seven miles to Columbine Campground on the left. From Eagle Nest, the campground is 5.2 miles on NM 38 E. From Questa, travel east on NM 38 for 4 miles just past Molycorp Mine, and look to right for Columbine Campground. There is parking in several places.

This is a beautiful, fairly easy hike through Columbine Canyon and is one of the most scenic hikes in the region.

You can do one of three hikes along this trail. Class 1 is a somewhat easy 4-mile round-trip that follows Columbine Creek with several footbridge crossings. Class 2 is 6 miles round-trip, but you'll have stream crossings. Class 3 is an 11-mile round-trip hike with the apex providing vistas of Taos Ski Valley. The trail does get steeper toward the end.

Chevron was busy dredging and relining adjacent Eagle Rock Lake. The river and stream projects were connected by a new trail system that created a unique angling opportunity. The nearby Red River that feeds the lake received instream habitat improvements along with riverside trails, footbridges, and other park amenities.

Camping in Questa–Red River

The campgrounds below are listed in order as you travel east from Questa on US 38; note that each of these sees heavy usage, especially between Memorial and Labor Days, so reservations are recommended. For more information, contact the Questa Ranger District at (575) 586-0520.

GOAT HILL

NM 38, Red River, NM 87558
(575) 586-0520
Six fee campsites, heavy usage, no water, one toilet. Tent and camper.

COLUMBINE CREEK

184 NM 38, Red River, NM 87558
(435) 245-6521
Four miles east of Questa. Twenty fee sites for tents or trailers, seven fee sites for trailers, heavy usage, water, several toilets, picnic tables.

LA BOBITA

NM 38, Red River, NM 87558
(575) 758-6200
An overflow campground, open only when needed.

ELEPHANT ROCK

745 E 200 S, Hyrum, NM 84319
(435) 245-6521
You can see a recent slide nearby. Twelve fee sites for tent or trailer camping, and ten fee sites for trailer only. Picnic tables, four toilets, drinking water, heavy usage.

FAWN LAKES

NM 38, Red River, NM 87558
(435) 245-6521
Twenty-two combined tent and trailer sites, picnic tables, toilets, drinking water, parking, heavy usage.

JUNE BUG

NM 38, Red River, NM 87558
(575) 586-0520
Two miles west of Red River. Fee tent and trailer camping, picnic tables, toilets, drinking water, parking.

Rio Grande del Norte National Monument

The Rio Grande del Norte National Monument was proclaimed a national monument March 25, 2013, by President Barack Obama. The monument encompasses the Rio Grande Gorge and surrounding lands, including adjacent Guadalupe Mountain. The Rio Grande del Norte National Monument is one of the wildest and most diverse areas of land in the country, with evidence everywhere of its geologic history. The landscape ranges from high-elevation wide open plains and deep river canyons to volcanic cones, natural hot springs, and riverine habitat.

The monument includes 242,555 acres of public land, most of which is managed by the Bureau of Land Management. The centerpiece is the Rio Grande, which has carved out an 800-foot deep gorge. Encompassing some of the most spectacular lands in America, the monument offers a wide range of outstanding recreational opportunities. It was designed to protect four key objects of value: geology, cultural and historic resources, ecological diversity, and wildlife. This means the area is closed for mining and related mineral and geothermal activities.

The Rio Grande del Norte National Monument is known for its geology, culture, natural history, and recreation.

The monument roughly covers the area between NM 522 and US 285 from Taos north to the state border. The area includes so many amazing places to see: the Wild Rivers Recreation Area, the Orilla Verde Recreation Area, and Taos Valley Overlook are all within the monument's boundary. The monument also includes Taos Junction Bridge, Rio Grande Gorge Visitor Center, Rio Grande Gorge High Bridge, John Dunn Bridge Recreation Site, Wild Rivers Area, Ute Mountain, Central Volcanoes Area, and Taos Plateau Prairie. This is one huge swath of land.

The mighty Rio Grande as it flows south from Colorado.

The northern portion of the monument crosses US 285, where you find the wide, gently rolling grass and sagebrush of the Rio San Antonio Wilderness Study Area. The most northwestern section of the monument includes the canyon, forest, and meadow stretches of the Rio de los Pinos, full of native Rio Grande cutthroat trout. The centerpiece (other than the Rio Grande, of course) of the monument might be Ute Mountain, a 10,093-foot-high volcanic cone rising strikingly several thousand feet above the surrounding plain.

The Orilla Verde Recreation Area (see page 81) and Taos Valley Overlook (see page 77) are accessed well south of this part of the monument.

The canyon ecosystem descends 800 feet from rim to river, creating a unique ecological diversity in plant and animal life, big mammals alongside small mammals. At rim level on the plains, you'll find ancient piñon and juniper forests that include five-hundred-year-old trees, but as you descend into the canyon, the biomes change and you'll find ponderosa pine and Douglas fir. This area has been beneficial to human activity since prehistoric times as evidenced by petroglyphs, prehistoric dwelling sites, and many other types of archaeological sites.

The climate of the area is semiarid with summer thunderstorms common in July and August, and snow possible from November through March. Summer temperatures range from forty-five to ninety degrees Fahrenheit and in winter from minus-fifteen to forty-five degrees. We've been in the canyon at times when it was warm enough for shirtsleeves only to meet up with snow by the time we reached the top of the trail.

The monument offers numerous activities including:

- whitewater rafting
- hunting
- fishing
- hiking
- cross-country skiing
- snowshoeing
- backpacking
- mountain biking
- birding
- rafting
- biking
- camping

What kind of animals can you hope to see? Rocky Mountain bighorn sheep, mule deer, Rocky Mountain elk, pronghorn antelope, the recently reintroduced North American river otter, Gunnison's prairie dog, ringtail, black bear, coyote, red fox, cougars, bobcats, red-tailed hawk, mountain blue-bird, trout (rainbow, brown, cutthroat), pike, and so many more. If you spend enough time in the monument, you'll see many of these.

The Rio Grande is part of the Central Migratory Flyway, an important migration corridor for birds. The basalt walls of the gorge are where eagles, falcons, and hawks make their homes. In and around the gorge, you might spot ospreys, herons, avocets, scaups, hummingbirds, Merlins, Willets, and even migrating sandhill cranes.

35

SIDE TRIP: **HIKE AT THE WILD RIVERS RECREATION AREA AT RIO GRANDE DEL NORTE MONUMENT**

Wild Rivers Visitor Center, 1120 Cerro Road
Cerro, NM 87519
(575) 586-1150 or (575) 758-8851
From Taos, go north on NM 522 through Questa; drive
3 miles beyond Questa and turn left (west) on NM 378.
You'll drive a good way, 17 miles, with lots of picnic areas
and trails and photo ops just off the road before you
get to the Wild Rivers Visitor Center.

This is dramatic country with the 800-foot canyon, wide desolate plains, evidence of ancient volcanic activity, and the confluence of the mighty Rio Grande and Red River. You can drive the Backcountry Byway, visit the visitor center, camp at the campgrounds, eat egg salad sandwiches at the picnic facilities, and hike the trails. Self-service permit pay stations are located at developed camping, picnic, and trailhead areas.

Wide open plains of the Rio Grande del Norte National Monument.

The Wild Rivers Recreation Area is in the upper portion of the Rio Grande del Norte National Monument and is approximately 14 miles north and turns later northwest of the Gorge Bridge; it includes a portion of the Rio Grande Wild and Scenic River and the Red River Wild and Scenic River. Wild Rivers offers a universally accessible visitor center, an overlook, picnic areas with tables and grills, drinking fountains, and restrooms. There are also two group shelters and five developed campgrounds. A few campsites, accessible only by hiking, are located at the bottom of the gorge. The visitor center is open daily during the summer and on holiday weekends during the winter. You will have so-so cell service surprisingly.

The 13-mile Wild Rivers Backcountry Byway is a paved driving loop that circles the entire recreation area. Within that loop is a graveled path that can be used for biking in the summer and cross-

---

Fees and Information about Wild Rivers Recreation Area

The Wild Rivers Recreation Area requires fees for day and overnight use.

Day use: $3 per day per vehicle to use the area for thirty minutes or more. An annual day use pass, good for the calendar year, is available for $20. The area is open year-round, 6:00 a.m.–10:00 p.m. An overnight camping fee will be required for anyone choosing to remain in the recreation area after the specified day use hours.

Camping: $7 per night for one vehicle, $10 for two. Maximum two vehicles and ten people per site. (Additional vehicles may park in day use parking areas at $3 per day.) Change is available at the visitor center or from a park ranger or camp host. Annual day use passes do not apply to camping fees.

River campsites: $5 per night.

Group shelters: $30 per day, $40 per night. Group shelters are by reservation—call the BLM Taos Field Office at (575) 758-8851.

country skiing in the winter. Along the rim are several easy trails including a half-mile-long interpretive trail.

The Wild Rivers Recreation Area has a dozen trails that descend from the rim of the gorge to the banks of the river, which offer some tough but excellent hikes. There are also trails along banks of the Rio Grande and some easier trails located atop the rim of the gorge. Two other access points to Wild Rivers include the Pescado Trail, which leaves from the visitor center and goes to the Red River Fish Hatchery, and the Cebolla Mesa Trail, which leaves from Forest Service lands south of the Red River and drops to the bank near the confluence of the Rio Grande and Red River.

Most popular trails in Wild Rivers

Several campgrounds are connected with the visitor center. You will see the trailheads at each campground.

RINCONADA LOOP TRAIL

Distance: 5-mile loop

Elevation gain: None

The Rinconada Loop Trail is a wide, all-weather-surface, beginner-level trail within Wild Rivers Recreation Area. This casual loop connects the several campgrounds with the visitor center. The gravel path is about 5 feet wide. Minimal elevation changes and a smooth tread make this easy in either direction. From the visitor center, the loop provides access to the Pescado Trail. Great for snowshoeing or cross-country skiing in winter and biking or hiking in summer.

BIG ARSENIC SPRINGS TRAIL

Distance: 2 miles round-trip

Elevation gain: 680 feet

This is a rock-walled trail with lots of switchbacks, steep in places but manageable, especially if you take your time, so use poles or walking sticks, and drink water. You will drop almost 700 feet into the canyon, but you'll gain access to the Rio Grande, the spring, petroglyphs, and great fishing. The trail has interpretive signs, benches, and lookouts, and you'll go from juniper and piñon to Douglas Fir and Ponderosa Pine.

About two-thirds of the way down, the trail splits. One path veers towards the Little Arsenic Springs Trail, and the other path (to the right) is the more well-known La Junta Trail. By the way, the name is misleading for Big and Little Arsenic springs. There is no arsenic. It's cold, clear spring water. But don't drink it. You might wonder why we haven't mentioned where to find the petroglyphs. They are intentionally unmarked to mitigate vandalism. Ask at the visitor center for directions.

LITTLE ARSENIC SPRINGS TRAIL

Distance: 1.8 miles round-trip
Elevation gain: 750 feet

This trail and the Big Arsenic Trail are on the southern loop of the Rio Grande del Norte National Monument. Another rock-walled hike, with lots of switchbacks and going a bit steeper than Big Arsenic, this trail takes about an hour down, two hours back out. There are picnic tables and shelters at the bottom. Eat there and visit the spring.

LA JUNTA TRAIL

Distance: 2.4 to 3 miles round-trip
Elevation gain: 800 feet

This centerpiece trail of the Wild Rivers Recreation Area, descending close to 800 feet into the canyon, is a 2.4-mile round-trip trail from La Junta Point to the dramatic confluence of the Rio Grande and the Red River. The mileage is debatable because you'll want to hike up or down the river a bit, so count on about 3 miles and know that the hike back up is steep and will take a lot longer than going down. At one point this trail requires the use of three sets of metal stairs and a short ladder to scale the near-vertical cliffs, which means coming up you'll have to climb the ladder. The trail also has lots of switchbacks.

The trail interconnects with a few other trails but this trail, as it is, is rated moderate. Don't go down unless you look at a good map to know that you could end up tying into one of the Arsenic trails. The Red River is blue and choppy, punctuated by big gray boulders and pocket water and springs that feed it. The Rio Grande is turbulent and powerful, with pocket water and riffles, long deep runs, and deeper pools. There are plenty of places to rest, eat your lunch, and take great photos.

La Junta trail leads to the confluence of the Rio Grande and Red River.

RED RIVER FAULT LOOP TRAIL

Distance: 5-mile loop

Elevation gain: 282 feet

This trail loops through piñon-juniper woods and across open sage flats providing nice views of Guadalupe Mountain.

Wild Rivers Visitor Center

The Wild Rivers Visitor Center provides information about recreation experiences as well as the geological and natural history of this diverse and interesting area. The visitor center is open Memorial Day through Labor Day, 10:00 a.m. until 4:00 p.m., with additional hours as staffing permits. After Labor Day, the visitor center is open as staffing permits.

Camping/Picnicking: Five campground areas are located at the Wild Rivers area. Each campground area is equipped with tables, grills, drinking water, and restroom facilities. There are two large group camping sites. In total, there are forty campsites available. Camping is permitted in designated sites only.

Trails: Most trails begin from campgrounds where day use parking spaces are provided. See the Wild Rivers Trail Map for trail locations (you can get these at the visitor center).

Biking: Unless signed otherwise, all roads on BLM lands are available for mountain biking. Please do not ride cross country. Three trails are open to mountain bikes: Rinconada Loop Trail, Red River Fault Trail, and Guadalupe Mountain Trail.

Campfires: Campfires are allowed in grills or firepans only. Camp stoves are recommended. Firewood collection is prohibited. Firewood is available for purchase at the visitor center or from a camp host. Please do not leave your fire unattended.

Pets: Pets must be kept under control and on a leash at all times. Pets are not permitted on Big Arsenic Trail or in freshwater springs.

36 SIDE TRIP: FISH AT VALLE VIDAL

Drive north from Questa, past Wild Rivers, almost to the Colorado border. Turn right at Costilla and go through Amalia. From Questa, drive north on NM 522 for nearly 20 miles, turn right at Costilla on NM 196 and continue for 25 miles. The last section of the road turns from paved to dirt.

If you are looking for incredible panoramic vistas of ancient volcanoes, pristine meadow streams that hold wild Rio Grande Cutthroat trout, look no further. Valle Vidal is one of the most beautiful places in the world. The isolated Rio Costilla runs for miles through a wide valley, curving back and forth through the caldera. The waters are clear, cold, and shallow, alternating between long, flat stretches, where the cutts hide under deep-cut banks, and foamy, deep bend pools, where the big trout lie in wait. The roads in are long and rough, preventing most anglers from making the trip. But the Rio Costilla is a special stream that simply cannot take the pounding of other streams—the trout and riparian habitats are too fragile. The river opens in early July to protect the spawning cutthroat and stays open until mid-December.

Latir Creek, one of the numerous fishing options in Valle Vidal.

Insider Tips and Information about Valle Vidal

When: The Valle Vidal section of the Rio Costilla opens July 1. Rio Costilla Cooperative Livestock Association (RCCLA) waters open in May, the lakes open mid to late June, depending on accessibility.

Where: Approximately 60 miles north of Taos.

Headquarters: Cimarron and McCrystal campgrounds, and Rio Costilla Park (primitive camping for a fee per night). Fishing on RCCLA land is about ten dollars per day, and if you fish outside their property, a state-issued license is required. You can camp on RCCLA land for a fee per car (about twenty dollars).

Appropriate gear: 3- and 4-weight rods, floating lines, 7.5- to 9-foot leaders, 4X and 5X tippets.

Useful fly patterns: Doc's Super Caddis, Witch Doctor, Terminator, Elk Hair Caddis, Goddard Caddis, Stimulator, Parachute Adams, hopper patterns, ant patterns, small bead-head nymphs.

Necessary accessories: Hip boots or wading boots/neoprene socks, polarized sunglasses, wide-brimmed hat, sunblock, first aid kit, water, emergency supplies, camping gear.

Find the brochure at riocostillapark.com/wp-content/uploads/2014/04/RCCLAbrochure.pdf.

Even though Valle Vidal is remote and isolated, a trip here is worth the effort. You have to want to go to the Valle Vidal; it's not something you pass through on the way to somewhere else.

The Valle Vidal Unit of the Carson National Forest consists of 100,000 acres between the villages of Cimarron and Costilla. Valle Vidal is a large grassy bowl rimmed by small rolling mountains covered in aspen and fir. Wildlife abounds in the unit, everything from rattlesnakes to elk, bison to bear, deer to the aforementioned wild trout.

Several trout streams run through this caldera but the two blue ribbons you'll want to concentrate on are tiny Comanche Creek and its bigger sister, Rio Costilla. Their confluence, with Comanche Peak standing sentinel over the junction, is the stuff postcards are made of.

Anglers will be rewarded with some of the best angling for wild cutthroats anywhere in the southwest. New Mexico Game and Fish electroshocking surveys show that over four thousand trout per mile inhabit these waters. The fish you're after? The rare Rio Grande cutthroat.

The Rio Grande cutthroat is one of the prettiest fish you'll ever catch. Their sides are splashed in aqua-green and royal purple. Their gills have been painted with iridescent blood-red slashes. In the water, against the pebbly bottom, they are invisible. In your hand, they are wiggling Monets. They average about eleven to fifteen inches long in the bigger water, and eight to twelve inches long in the lesser water. You will catch Rio Grande cutts, hybrids (rainbows breeding with cutts), and rainbows. Regulations protect the cutthroats, and it's a good thing too. Rio Grande Cutthroats inhabit less than 7 percent of their original habitat.

Comanche Creek is a step-across stream snaking through open fields, a tiny trickle of water that at first looks like it doesn't even hold trout. Bully for you, it does. Let others bypass this gem. That's the beauty of this narrow meandering creek—no one bothers to fish it. The Comanche holds plenty of Rio Grande cutthroats ranging from fit-in-your-palm to wow-I-had-no-idea-that-size-fish-lurked-in-here (roughly translated, that means the fish range from six inches to fourteen inches). Fish Comanche as stealthily as you would if you were stealing your sister's diary while she sleeps, or you'll quickly be discovered by these stealthy trout.

Downstream from the National Forest boundary, Rio Costilla flows through about 6 miles of RCCLA property. Much of this stretch is canyon water. Steep granite walls drop straight down to the deepest parts of the Rio Costilla. Rather than the typical canyon stream characterized by gushing stair-step pools and riffles, this canyon-bound stretch of river presents odd swirling pools, dips and dives under overhanging limbs; anglers must continually combat

The rare Rio Grande cutthroat.

the riparian trees and brush, including tangles of alders along with evergreens. It's a quirky place to fish. The low-slung green mountains that rise gently up from the caldera through which the Rio Costilla runs will remind you of Paradise Valley in Yellowstone National Park.

The RCCLA property boasts a new camping and RV area along the Costilla about halfway between Latir Creek and the Valle Vidal border. On RCCLA land, you can also camp at primitive campsites. High up in the RCCLA property, nine watery gems collectively known as the Latir Lakes are loaded with big trout (stocked on a rotating basis). Talk to anyone who's fished the lakes over the last decade or two and you'll inevitably hear about some of the huge cutts and cuttbows caught (or just spotted) in these lakes. The largest pair of these lakes span perhaps six to eight acres and most cover just one to three acres, making them perfect for fly fishing. Think scuds and midges. The lakes tentatively open the middle of June or first of July, depending on the road conditions and the spawning of native trout. Contact the RCCLA office at (575) 586-0542 to confirm that the lakes are open and accessible.

Angler casting on Little Blue Lake.

A new access road now reaches the Latir Lakes; it branches off from the road to Little Blue Lake. Follow the signs, and be aware that while the new road is an improvement over the old road and you can take a passenger car (many do), we still recommend a high-clearance vehicle. You can hike to the lower lakes but most will drive up. Consider toting in a float tube because trees line the banks of most of the lakes. A well-marked hiking trail now ties into the existing Falls Trail.

Shuree Ponds are best fished with nymphs and streamers. Some anglers make the long drive into Valle Vidal just to fish these three lakes. The water is clear and the big trout look like cruising submarines. The rainbows and hybrid Rio Grande cutthroat in Shuree Ponds dwarf those you'll have been catching in the river.

OTHER THINGS
to See and Do from Questa to Red River

CABRESTO LAKE AND CREEK

From the stoplight in Questa (there is only one), go east on NM 38 toward Red River. After about 0.6 miles, you'll see a green sign indicating Cabresto Lake. Turn left (north) at the sign onto Kiowa Road. Stay on this road for about 2.2 miles where it dead-ends into a T-intersection. Turn right onto FR 134. Drive about 3.4 miles on FR 134. You will see a sign pointing left and indicating Cabresto Lake is 2 miles away on FR 134A. This road gains a lot of elevation and is rough, narrow, and winding. No camp trailers are allowed. Drive on FR 134A for 2.1 miles and when the road ends and you'll know you've reached the campground and lake.

The campground (9,283 feet) is primitive and has a few established campsites, one vault toilet, no running water, and amazing views. Even though the road is difficult and narrow, you'll see lots of traffic in the small parking area. You will also see a few passenger cars. A 4WD vehicle makes it up to the lake with no problem, and the road doesn't get muddy even in hard rain. But we recommend a high-clearance 4WD vehicle anyway. The lake has cutthroat and brook trout. Fishing the creek is hard because it's small and brushy, and in many places no trail exists. Lake Fork Creek feeds into Cabresto Lake and Creek.

HEART LAKE

Distance: 9 miles round-trip from Cabresto Lake
(also known as Lake Fork Trail)

Elevation gain: 2,300 feet

Trailhead: The trailhead lies left (west) of Cabresto Lake.

Heart Lake (11,500 feet) is located about 4.5 miles from Cabresto Lake via the Heart Lake Trail. The trail has a steady uphill gradient and goes through dense forest with a small meadow here and there. A creek runs alongside the trail. Heart Lake Trail 85 can be accessed from Cabresto Lake Trail 82 or Midnight Trail 81. From Cabresto Lake, follow Lake Fork Trail 82 for 4 miles, passing the Bull Creek Trail 85. After the log crossing

Ute Mountain is a sentinel on the open prairie.

there are a few campsites that mark a halfway point. Continue the moderate trail making a left at the intersection of Heart Lake Trail 85 and Baldy Trail 81. From there hike a half-mile to Heart Lake.

UTE MOUNTAIN

After you visit the Wild Rivers Recreation Area, continue north on NM 522. You will cross just over the state line in Colorado. Turn left on County Road B toward the village of Jaroso. Turn south and follow the signs into the Ute Mountain Area.

At 10,093 feet, Ute Mountain is the highest point of the Rio Grande del Norte National Monument. The rugged volcanic mountain juts dramatically nearly 3,000 feet up from the sage flats and grasslands at its base just south of the Colorado border. The striking rise offers a remarkable contrast to the nearby gorge cutting along its western flank.

Ute and the surrounding volcanic cones are relics of an age when the Rio Grande Rift valley spread and created massive lava flows across the plateau. The craggy landscape, free of designated trails, provides fabulous primitive recreational opportunities and some of the best stargazing skies in the nation.

Sharp elevation gain along the forested slopes of the mountain creates a great diversity of wildlife habitat. The steep slopes of Ute Mountain are covered in piñon at the base just above grassy meadows of blue grama, western wheatgrass, and Indian ricegrass. The climb brings you into pockets of ponderosa, aspen, white pine, and Douglas fir in the higher elevations where the trees thin and the sky opens to a one-of-a-kind vista. Beware of rattlesnakes and prickly vegetation. Be sure to bring plenty of water.

CARSON NATIONAL FOREST

You'll see signs for entering or leaving Carson National Forest all over northern New Mexico and with good reason—Carson National Forest encompasses 1.5 million acres. The Forest Service's mixed-use policy allows its use for recreation, grazing, and resource extraction. The Carson National Forest is one of five National Forests in New Mexico.

Elevations rise from 6,000 feet to 13,161 feet at Wheeler Peak, the highest in New Mexico. Recreation includes fishing, hunting, camping, and hiking. Winter activities include skiing, snowshoeing, and snowmobiling.

A sign to Carson National Forest, home to the most impressive scenery in the Southwest.

FROM RED RIVER
TO EAGLE NEST

RED RIVER

Route: Leave Questa on NM 38 east, and drive 12.2 miles to
Red River (18 minutes).
Elevation: 8,671 feet
Population: 477
Lay of the land: high mountain, alpine, lots of pines,
spruce, and aspens

Red River is a scenic former mining town set right in the middle of
mountains. You can walk easily from one end of town to the other.
You'll see lots of families in this wholesome, 1950s-feel, clean-air, tidy
little snow village. Red River hasn't changed all that much in the last
four decades.

The town originally boomed in the late 1800s as a worthwhile
location for miners hunting gold and trappers seeking game. The last
earnest attempts at mining extended through the early 1930s, but
for the last eighty-five or so years Red River's main draw has been
tourism, an oasis for mountainous exploration and relaxation. Red
River is blessed with over three hundred days of sunshine a year, with
great skiing in winter, trout fishing, and four-wheeling in summer.

Transportation

Red River's public transportation is called the Miner's Transit and
will take you throughout Red River free of charge. They operate
every day and are especially popular with skiers going from their
lodging right to the slopes. Traveling to and from Albuquerque?
Ask about their longer ride service by calling (575) 770-5959.
Find more at redriver.org/town/transportation.

*Top, left to right: Artistic signage in town; Goose Lake (Photo credit: Heritage
Inspirations Travel.). Bottom: Frye's Old Town in Red River.*

Red River runs right through town. It's the reason this town exists: from the Apaches and Utes who frequented the area in the 1800s, to the pioneers to the fur trappers to the prospectors, to the river, flowing from the northern slope of Wheeler Peak—all of this contributes to the lifeblood of the community. The village was in fact originally called River City.

Like many Western boomtowns of the nineteenth century, when the mining for copper, silver, and gold was good, the town was hopping and populated, complete with saloons and gambling halls, as well as a sawmill, blacksmith, barbershop, two newspapers, livery stable, two general mercantile stores, and a red-light district.

When the mining ran dry by 1905, miners left in search of the next get-rich-quick boomtown (one more surge of mining petered out by the 1930s). With excellent trout fishing and cool summers, tourism followed. The ski resort opened in the 1950s (a family-owned business, of course). Red River became a great home base for outdoor recreation year-round. Snowy and white in winter, cool and green in summer, Red River has been a vacation destination for decades. Families have been coming here for vacation since the 1940s, and you'll find that folks from Oklahoma and Texas are the main visitors. From zip-lining to fly fishing, the town of Red River offers countless activities for every season. Check the Visitor's Center at 101 West River Street, Red River, NM 87558, or call (575) 754-3030 for information.

Red River loves its festivals. Music, arts and crafts, food, the town has a seasonal festival about something seemingly almost every week (check the calendar at redriver.org/events). What else to do in Red River if you're tired from all the outdoor activities? Try shopping, restaurants and bars, various stores, the great park, or take a stroll along the trail that follows this gorgeous mountain stream. Remember that this is high elevation, so don't exert yourself until you're acclimated and drink plenty of water.

For a little history, check out Red River's buildings on the National Register of Historical Places at redriver.org/town/history-facts/history.

The Little Red School House Museum has photos, artifacts, and a classroom setting, with items from the Red River Historical Society. The building was the town's school from around 1915 to 1942 and then became an integral part of the town as a community hall. Admission is free, but donations are accepted, which help this little museum stay up and running. A couple of historic cabins and several pieces of mining equipment are housed outside the museum. A few other cabins can be investigated through the Red River Community House's Historical Tours. Call (575) 754-2349 for information.

Looking for Something Different to Do in Red River?

- Go for a chuckwagon dinner and entertainment from Michael Martin Murphey's Rockin' 3M Chuckwagon Suppers at the amphitheater. Call (575) 754-6280 for tickets.
- Buy some fudge from the candy store.
- Visit the Red River Community House (116 East Main Street, Red River, NM 87558; (575) 754-2349) and take one of their guided hikes.
- Have a streamside picnic.
- Take one of the Bobcat Pass Wilderness Adventure trips. Call (575) 754-2769 to book a trip.
- Show off your free-skiing and snowboarding skills with "rail jams" before torchlight parades and fireworks on Saturdays and special holidays. See the events calendar at redriverskiarea.com/.

Alpine village nestled in the Sangre de Cristo Mountains.

Red River embraces the idea that here's where the Old West meets modern ski resort. Beyond the western facades, signage, and trimmings throughout Red River, the town even has a cheesy Old West shootout in summer at Frye's Old Town (100 West Main Street, Red River, NM 87558; (575) 754-3028) where the law tries to thwart a bank robbery. This good-guys-versus-bad-guys shootout is a fun Red River tradition, entertaining families and going strong since the 60s. Some critics say that Red River feels awfully touristy and tacky with its souvenir and curio shops, but we like the locally owned, family-based businesses. Yes, you can find numerous shops that sell T-shirts and caps, that sort of thing, but there is a wide variety of fun and interesting products and services up and down the main drag.

A wintry look at Main Street and Red River Ski Area from Frye's Old Town.

You are likely to see deer milling around in the street or in the yards, but there are also bears at night so don't leave food out. If you leave food outside where they can smell it or get to it, well, you've got a problem. Not many ski resorts in New Mexico have the ski resort in the town itself—the ski resorts are usually a few miles from the actual town—so Red River is unusual in that respect.

38 EXPLORE RED RIVER SKI & SUMMER AREA

400 Pioneer Road, Red River, NM 87558
(575) 754-2223
redriverskiarea.com/
Toward the north end of town (near Shotgun Willie's),
Pioneer Road intersects with Main Street.
Turn south on Pioneer Road. Red River Ski Area
is at the end of Pioneer Road.

Red River is known by many as the "Ski Town of the Southwest." It's been a popular wintertime playground since the official Red River Ski Area opened in 1959. Skiers and snowboarders have access to multi-level terrain that's pretty evenly split among beginner, intermediate, and advanced levels. If you're a newbie, or if you just want to improve, sign up for ski or snowboard lessons to make the most out of your time here (you can book reservations online). In no time you'll have the knowledge for exploring the mountain along with everyone else. One of the best parts of Red River Ski Area is that it's part of the town. You can access lifts just a hop, skip, and a jump off of Main Street.

Christmastime is a fun, magical experience in Red River with the Christmas Eve torchlight parade and fireworks celebration. Other fun events include Mardi Gras celebrations in February and March's Beach Week where you just may see hula skirts and bikini tops on the slopes. Every Saturday night during ski season is a celebration with a torchlight parade and fireworks. Red River loves to celebrate.

The ski area also has fun tubing runs for the whole family. Get your ticket early (you can make reservations three days in advance) as the spots fill up quickly. One ticket gives you an hour's worth of riding.

While the town's ski area gets top billing for winter fun, there are lots of other options in and around Red River for enjoying the snow.

Snowshoeing and Nordic skiing fans often head to Enchanted Forest (see page 200) or to other outlying trails around town. If you want something faster, then look into renting a snowmobile for the day and zooming through some beautiful scenery.

The ski lifts are right beside the river.

(You'll need a permit as well. Find more information at redriver.org/things-to-do/winter-recreation/snowmobiling-ohv.) Snowcat rentals are available too for a fun backcountry guided tour. There are places in town to rent gear, including snowshoes and sleds. Ask shops for specifics, but popular snowshoeing trails include Pioneer Canyon and the Nature Trail. Sledders often head to the area near St. Edwin's Catholic Church and Mallette Park. If you bring your own snowmobile, be sure to be properly licensed and have proper permits. Groomed trails run in the Valle Vidal (once the elk have moved) to Greenie Peak, and from the Upper Red River Valley to Middle Fork Lake. For an

The ski mountain is great for leaf-peeping opportunities.

evening experience, take Red River's Snow Coach Dinner Tour (redriverskiarea.com/winter/dinner/) up to the 10,350-foot summit for a beautiful evening and a delicious meal. A round-trip ride takes about two hours. Call Red River Guest Services for reservations.

Of course, it's easy to have winter fun in Red River without making much of a plan. Build a snowman, throw snowballs, or huddle up by a fire and roast marshmallows and drink something warm. Check the winter calendar of events at redriverskiarea.com/events/things-to-do-in-winter/.

But the Red River Ski Area is lovely in the summer as well. There's not much as refreshing as Red River's cool, summertime mountain air. Daytime temperatures rarely reach into the eighties, making it a vacationer's dream, especially when filled with loads of fun and natural beauty.

Summer brings a transformation to the wintertime ski resort with all sorts of activities for young and old. Something all ages can enjoy is the scenic chairlift ride (redriverskiarea.com/summer/activities/scenic-chairlift-ride/) that whisks guests up to the mountain's summit of 10,350 feet. The stunning views of Carson National Forest give that I'm-on-top-of-the-world feeling. Ride the lift right back down (about an hour round-trip) or hop off and have lunch at the mountain's

Red River Ski Area Stats

Average annual snowfall: 214 inches

Average days of sunshine: 300+ days

Base elevation: 8,750 feet

Summit elevation: 10,350 feet

Vertical drop: 1,600 feet

Number of trails: 63 total: 32% beginner, 38% intermediate, 30% advanced

Number of lifts: 1 quad, 3 triples, 1 double, 2 surface lifts

Terrain parks: 3 total: Hollywood, Pot O' Gold, and Snowcross.

Glade skiing: 1 glade

Snowmaking capabilities: 85% of the mountain

Skiable acreage: 290 acres

—from Red River Ski Resort, redriverskiarea.com/

restaurant then take a guided nature walk (redriverskiarea.com/summer/activities/hiking/) for interesting details on the mountain's history and environment. If you like to set out independently, choose a trail and hike back to the base at your own leisure.

Mountain biking enthusiasts have a full mountain to explore and plenty of places to catch some air. Pack your wheels on the lift for a quick ride up, or if you've got calves of steel, pedal up the mountain. Note that this mountain bike trek is not for beginners; the trails are suited for intermediate to advanced riders.

Another summit option is the eighteen-hole disc golf course which is free for those who bike or hike to the top. Get in some good practice then come back for the fall disc golf tournament. Lift passes can be purchased for one trip up or for the entire day.

Not to let winter tubing have all the fun, Red River offers up excitement on their summer tubing lanes made of a specially designed hard plastic (redriverskiarea.com/summer/activities/summer-mountain-tubing/). Options include tubing Baby Blue hill for the littles or one of the longest summer tubing hills around, Gold Rush Hill. If you ride down Gold Rush on your own, be prepared for your tube to spin you round and round as you head down; or, for a more straightforward descent, link your tube to a buddy's.

Near the base of the slopes, don't miss one of the most thrilling summer activities. The Hidden Treasure Aerial Park (redriverskiarea. com/summer/activities/hidden-treasure-aerial-park/) offers three levels of challenge-course adventure ranging from easiest to most difficult. Courses take thrill seekers along ziplines and through all kinds of ropes courses high up in the air.

The Pioneer Flyer (redriverskiarea.com/summer/activities/pioneer-flyer/) offers up another thrilling zip with a 35-miles-per-hour flight over the fishing ponds. Riders have to be at least forty-two inches tall to be buckled in and pulled back seven hundred and fifty feet then released for the speedy ride.

Besides all the summer action at the ski mountain, Red River guests can explore the town on foot or by family pedal cart, walk the river trail, play in the park, have a picnic, cool off in the river, or give fishing a try. Four-wheeling is popular with lots of places to challenge your vehicle. All-terrain vehicles have numerous roads to play too. For 4WD and ATV action, check with local rental companies.

Plenty of special summer events and live music fun keep visitors entertained. Check the calendar at redriverskiarea.com/events/things-to-do-in-summer/. Remember that while the summer weather is fab here, the sun's rays are intense and you can still get a sunburn and exposure to harmful UV rays, so bring sunscreen and a hat.

39 FISH RED RIVER

It's not as easy as just saying, "go fish Red River." Pick your section. You can fish all through town and a walking trail follows much of it. You'll catch mostly stocked rainbow trout in water that has thankfully seen instream rehabilitation. It's often crowded during the summer.

Fishing Red River in the canyon.

The best water is the 4 miles from the Red River Fish Hatchery (see page 150) downstream to its confluence with the Rio Grande. In summer, when the heat is brutal, the canyon is cool and hidden from the oven above. Descending along developed trails into the basalt-walled canyon is a strenuous hike. The views of the heavily bouldered freestone river are eye catching. There are some whoppers in those deep stairstep pools. You can catch brown, cutthroat, rainbow, and occasionally brook trout.

The river is frequently stocked and has some nice-sized trout. Most of the trout will be catchable size (eight to twelve inches). Don't expect to fish alone because in summer there's always someone in the water or at a good pool. The trick is to move up and down away from the other folks and find your own spot. The river is good for spin and fly fishing and has a lot of instream rehabilitation so there's lots of holding water. A trail runs beside the river.

The best equipment to use for fly fishing are 7.5- to 8.5-foot rods for 3- to 5-weight line. Hip waders are handy but hiking while wearing waders is bound to be uncomfortable. Anglers might consider wearing hiking boots with a lightweight pair of wading boots and breathable waders packed in a daypack. If you do hike in waders, be forewarned they could easily get torn up from rocks and brush.

For anybody who has fished for big fish moving up from the Rio Grande in the fall and spring, you know this hard-to-get-to fishery is one of the best secrets in New Mexico. And despite the crowds around the hatchery, the fishing is usually productive, especially in the canyon's stairstep pools below.

Make sure to visit the public sections of the headwaters south of Red River as winter turns into spring and then again when the snow has melted.

Mountain Biking around Red River

Red River offers several mountain biking paths including Old Red River Pass Road, Fourth of July Canyon, Midnight Meadows, Middle Fork Lake, Pioneer Canyon Trail, Enchanted Forest Cross-Country Ski Area, Goose Lake, up in Valle Vidal, Costilla Pass, and Rock Wall Loop. Visit redriver.org/things-to-do/summer-recreation/mountain-biking for more information.

HIKES
around Red River

RED RIVER NATURE TRAIL

Distance: 4 miles round-trip

Elevation gain: None

Trailhead: At the Red River Ski Area Platinum Lift on Pioneer Road.

This is a popular, easy walk right beside the river and through town. The Red River Nature Trail starts at the Platinum Lift on Pioneer Road and mostly follows the river for 2 miles to Goose Lake Road. This trail features trailside interpretive signs.

If you'd like to walk another short trail, try the quarter-mile nature loop along the creek in Mallette Park (on the opposite side of Main Street from the ski area).

GOOSE CREEK (AND GOOSE LAKE) TRAIL 65

Distance: 14.7 miles round-trip

Elevation gain: 2,700 feet

Trailhead: Drive south of Red River on NM 38 and turn right (south) on Goose Lake Road (FR 486). Go a little over 2 miles to the Goose Creek trailhead on right and park.

Hike across the bridge and veer left along Red River. You'll see the Goose Creek Trail on the right. Take this trail 7 miles to Goose Lake. There are two river crossings and meadow and forest sections, and it's moderately steep in places.

Hiking to Goose Creek on a beautiful day.

BULL OF THE WOODS TRAIL

Distance: 7.5 miles one-way to summit of Wheeler Peak, 15 miles round-trip

Elevation gain: 3,686 feet (trailhead elevation: 9,475 feet; summit elevation: 13,161 feet)

Trailhead: Start at the Taos Ski Valley parking lot near the picnic area off of the upper lot. Make sure you have good maps and GPS because there are some tricky spots.

The Bull of the Woods Trail is a trail running from the Taos Ski Valley parking lot to the Bull of the Woods Mountain. A scenic pause is the Bull of the Woods pasture, which is approximately 2 miles from the start. Horses and hikers use this trail (no bikes).

The ascent to Wheeler Peak is not for the beginner because this is often a steep and challenging trail. Just going up to the pasture is steep and challenging with a rate of 680 feet gain per mile. When you get to the pasture, the trail meets with several trails (Gold Hill Trail, Goose Lake Trail, and Forest Trail 175) from Red River and continues to the Wheeler Peak Trail (TR 90). Many go up the Bull of the Woods trail and down the Williams Lake Trail for an 11.5-mile round-trip adventure.

MIDDLE FORK LAKE FR 487

Distance: 4 miles round-trip

Elevation gain: 1,600 feet

Trailhead: Travel south from Red River on NM 38 and turn right (south) on NM 578 and drive 6.4 miles to the end of the pavement. Turn onto the gravel road, FR 58, and drive another 1.3 miles to the parking area. This is the trailhead for both Lost Lake and Middle Fork Lake Trails.

You don't have to use a high-clearance vehicle or a 4WD vehicle to get here, but we do, and we recommend them. This is a moderate hike that follows the Middle Fork Creek to Middle Fork Lake, a scenic, fishable mountain lake (New Mexico Game and Fish stocks it with rainbow trout in summer).

HORSESHOE LAKE 91 AND EAST FORK TRAIL 56

Distance: 12 miles round-trip

Elevation gain: 2,630 feet

Trailhead: Travel south from Red River on NM 578 (old NM 150) about 6 miles to the Middle Fork and East Fork junction. The pavement ends here. Turn left onto FR 58A; cross the bridge and travel approximately 1.25 miles to the wilderness users parking area.

Horseshoe Lake Trail is a moderately trafficked out-and-back trail located near Red River that features a lake and is only recommended for very experienced adventurers. This trail ties into the hike to Wheeler Peak (adds 4 miles more to your round-trip). The lake (11,950 feet) is at timberline and has ancient bristlecone pine shrubs you should not damage. Camp at least 300 feet away from lake. Horseshoe Lake is stocked every few years by helicopter with native cutthroat fry. A fishing license and trout stamp are required in New Mexico.

LOST LAKE TRAIL 91

Distance: 11 miles round-trip

Elevation gain: 2,299 feet

Trailhead: Travel south from Red River on NM 38 and turn right (south) on NM 578 and drive 6.4 miles to the end of the pavement. Turn onto the gravel road, FR 58, and drive another 1.3 miles to the parking area for Middle Fork/Lost Lakes Trails. Like Middle Fork trail, you will hike up the jeep trail for a quarter-mile to a gate. Turn left, cross Red River by bridge for a mile; turn left on Lost Lake Trail 91 and hike to Lost Lake for a couple of miles. You will reach Lost Lake, beautifully cobalt-blue, and on its western side you can find a small waterfall. This is high country so watch out for summer storms and lightning. The lake is stocked with cutthroat trout via helicopter every few years.

40 SNOWSHOE AT THE ENCHANTED FOREST CROSS COUNTRY SKI AREA

29 Sangre de Cristo Drive, Red River, NM 87558
(575) 754-6112
Pay a visit to this little piece of heaven just 3 miles east of Red River on NM 38. You'll turn right (south) onto Sangre de Cristo just after mile marker 16, a little past the Enchanted Forest sign. Keep going up the mountain for about a mile and you'll see the first parking area.

The Enchanted Forest Cross Country Ski Area, just outside Red River, is the place in New Mexico for Nordic skiing and snowshoeing fans. Started in 1989 by the present owner's father, the Enchanted Forest is the only place in the state exclusively designed for Nordic skiing and snowshoeing. A big bonus to this beautiful segment of the Carson National Forest is the placement of two yurts for overnight lodging along the trails. This popular glamping opportunity is available in both summer and winter and make for great stargazing nights and adventuring along the trails when the moon's bright.

Trails here have a secluded wilderness feel and are well marked and groomed with just enough uphill and downhill stretches to suit all levels and to cater to everyone's tastes. For winter adventurers, classic and Nordic skiers have at least 18 miles of wide trails to choose from and snowshoeing enthusiasts have 9-plus miles of trails to explore. The owners of Enchanted Forest have even considered four-legged pals and have 3 miles of trails set aside just for you and your pooch. Besides Enchanted's groomed trails, you have access to loads of backcountry paths as well. If you're a fat-tire bike rider, ask what snowy trails are available for you. You can bike ride in the summer too.

No matter how you explore these high-altitude wilderness trails during the winter, keep an eye out for the quiet animals that call this place home. Maybe you'll see a deer or a snowshoe hare. Soak in the beauty and listen to the quiet of the forest. And be sure to look for

Cross-country skiing through the Enchanted Forest's winter wonderland. (Photo credit: Enchanted Forest Cross Country Ski Area.)

views of Wheeler Peak in the distance. Popular wintertime events include traversing the beautiful luminaria-lit trails on Christmas night. This event is a fun and magical way to wind down after all the Christmas hubbub. Christmas night guests have access to the warming hut, free posole, cookies, and hot drinks.

Later, in February, is a sweet event with dessert tastings from local restaurants set up along the trails. Ski or snowshoe a little, then eat a little, and so on. Winter at the Enchanted Forest brings visitors of all ages. Little ones can even ride in a pulk (small sled) behind a parent. They're surprisingly easy to pull as long as your kiddo and any gear weigh under sixty pounds. Kids age five and under are admitted free and seniors seventy and older get a special discount.

Summer at the Enchanted Forest begins on June 1st with the warm weather activities of hiking and biking. The best part is that there is no trail fee for hikers and bikers throughout the summertime. Special events include full-moon hikes, trail running/fitness camps for women, mountain biking clinics, and even interpretive astronomy evenings. They also host running and cycling races along their summertime trails. Keep an eye on their calendar at enchantedforestxc.com/ for updates and details on the fun.

If you want to secure a yurt for one of your excursions, book it early. They fill up quickly. Yurts are furnished with beds, wood stoves, and cooking utensils, but you'll need to pack all your own gear including a sleeping bag and water. Rent a pulk to pull your goods, or pay a little extra and have sled delivery to your yurt. You can't drive to any of the yurts, and the closest one is about a mile in. Note that dogs are not allowed overnight during the winter months.

Contact the Enchanted Forest for fees and reservations, or if you need help with directions or anything else. The staff is known for being friendly and helpful.

41 WANDER IN GHOST TOWN ELIZABETHTOWN

After coming down from Bobcat Pass you'll be just a few miles from the Enchanted Circle's ghost town. Around mile marker 20 (before you get to the cutoff for Elizabethtown) look right for a glimpse of a colorful, folk-art serpent bridge. Before you know it, there'll be an old, wooden, faded sign off to the left for Elizabethtown. We've passed it and had to turn around before. The sign is on the left, but the turn for E-town is to the right (south). Turn right onto Elizabethtown Overlook Road; drive less than a mile to the ghost town. Park anywhere you want off the road.

Present-day ghost town Elizabethtown, New Mexico, isn't much more than a spot in the road, but it houses a breadth of history from a Ute Indian gifting William H. Moore with copper-filled rocks to that of a local serial killer.

Elizabethtown reached its peak population of seven thousand back in 1870 with residents hopeful of scoring pockets full of gold

The cutoff to Elizabethtown is easy to miss, but once you turn and see the railroad crossing sign you'll know you're on the right path.

from the area's mines. This burgeoning town was founded by Captain William Moore after his scouting crew sought out more of the pretty copper rocks and ended up discovering gold. Elizabethtown, named after Moore's young daughter, had more than a hundred buildings at its peak, including hotels, saloons, churches, and dance halls. Moore and his brother owned and operated the general store and the town built up around it.

While Moore gets a lot of credit for starting the town, it was really due to the Ute Indians he befriended. First they asked to trade the pretty, copper-filled rocks for supplies from Captain Moore at nearby Fort Union. Later, Moore ended up saving the life of his Ute Indian friend, who in return gave Moore the mineral-rich rocks and showed him where they came from, high on the upper slope of Mt. Baldy. Hence, the gold mining days in the area began. Lucien Maxwell actually owned the land at that time, but once the gilded secret was out, there was no stopping gold-hungry hopefuls from staking their claim. Maxwell ended up charging fees to the miners, which some paid and some did not. In the end, Maxwell joined in the gold exploration with Moore, and they started their own mining company.

Elizabethtown has seen its share of outlaws, Indian raids, and harsh winters. But the biggest hardship story people talk about is that of E-town's own serial killer. Apparently Charles Kennedy ran an overnight house and didn't let most of his visitors leave. He'd rob them and kill them, then either burn or bury the bodies. His sordid secret was safe until his Ute wife escaped her likely death after he killed their child and another visitor. Kennedy was captured by the vigilantes of the time, who took matters into their own hands. They abducted Kennedy from the jail, put a noose around his neck, and dragged him back and forth through town long after he'd met his demise.

As was typical of gold mining, the gold rush didn't last, and neither did the gold-mining town of Elizabethtown. Within a couple of years, the population plummeted to only a hundred or so residents. In the 1890s, the Atchison Topeka and Santa Fe Railroad passed nearby E-town and settlers started returning to this once lively settlement. Unfortunately, E-town took another hit when the fire of 1903 devoured most of the town, causing most who were left to make a move to the new Eagle Nest Lake. The local Muntz hotel was rebuilt out of stone, but the town just couldn't recover, and by 1917 the town was practically void of townsfolk and miners. But Elizabeth Moore, the town's namesake, lived her entire life in E-town and even became the town's first school teacher.

Ruins of the old ghost town.

FROM
EAGLE NEST
TO ANGEL FIRE

EAGLE NEST

Route: Leave Red River on NM 38 east,
  drive 17.4 miles to Eagle Nest.
Elevation: 8,090 feet
Population: 189
Lay of the land: valley and lake

Let's get this out of the way—it's Eagle Nest, not Eagle's Nest. You'll sound just like a local if you get this right.

Eagle Nest, the "Gateway to the Enchanted Circle," lies on the easternmost point of the circle and is a sleepy, fairly undiscovered village in Moreno Valley, with its centerpiece the big blue Eagle Nest Lake (2,200 acres) and the mountains that circle it, especially the sentinel peaks of Wheeler and Baldy. The village sits at 8,382 feet above sea level, so the village enjoys cool, dry summers and snowy winters. In the summer, temperatures range from a high of mid-eighties to a low of mid-thirties. In the winter the temperature range is from a high of mid-forties to a low of minus-ten degrees Fahrenheit. Snowfall is fairly heavy, averaging 62.8 inches and getting as deep as 150 inches.

Like all the towns of the Enchanted Circle, Eagle Nest has a rich and interesting history. In 1918, the Cimarron River was dammed for irrigation purposes to create Eagle Nest Lake. A new town named Therma sprung up. As Elizabethtown, Baldy City, and other mining towns quit producing, those residents moved to Therma. Tourists started coming to the town over the next two decades, and by the mid-1930s Therma was renamed Eagle Nest, for the lake. Now here's where it gets interesting: during the early years and into the 1940s, Eagle Nest was so isolated that you could still come to town and enjoy slot machines, gaming tables, and ladies-of-the-night in several establishments, especially the El Monte Hotel (now the Laguna Vista).

Top: the town streets of Eagle Nest. Bottom: options for drivers into Eagle Nest.

Finally, the law came down on the illegal and open gambling and prostitution rackets of Eagle Nest and closed them.

Today you can stroll the sidewalks up and down the main street and find flower boxes, old-timey street lights, and self-guided historical markers in addition to the restaurants and stores. Because the town still has the Old West feel, you can imagine yourself back in time.

Looking for Something Different to Do in Eagle Nest?

- Go to the summertime Farmers' Market at 540 West Therma, Eagle Nest, NM 87718, open mid-June to August.
- Visit the Enchanted Circle Gateway Museum at 580 East Therma Drive (US 64), Eagle Nest, NM 87718.
- Watch the Fourth of July fireworks display.
- Attend the July High Country Arts Festival in late July.
- Look for the valley's elk herd. They move around but you can often see them grazing.
- Go birding at the lake for duck, geese, pelicans, herons, crows, ospreys, or the year-round songbirds.
- People who stay at the Laguna Vista Lodge (51 East Therma Drive, Eagle Nest, NM 87718; (575) 377-6522) swear that a ghost haunts its halls. She wears a dance-hall dress and disappears into a hidden staircase when people get a glimpse of her. The rumor is that her husband abandoned her in Eagle Nest and she became a dance-hall girl as she still pines for her long-lost husband. If you like that sort of thing, go in and see what you can discover.

BOAT AT EAGLE NEST LAKE

Eagle Nest Lake State Park, 42 Marina Way,
Eagle Nest, NM 87718
(575) 377-1594
You can get to the lake several ways but to enter by
the state park, head south from Eagle Nest on US 64;
drive 7 miles and turn left on Elk Lane Road.

42

The main draw of Eagle Nest is the big, beautiful, blue 2,200-acre man-made namesake lake. Wheeler Peak, New Mexico's highest mountain, rises in the background above the lake and the town sits on the north side of Eagle Nest Lake in a glacial valley. The lake itself is a man-made reservoir created when the Cimarron River was impounded by the Eagle Nest Dam in 1918. Catch a great fireworks show on Independence Day each year. The mountains in the background and the shimmering lake below reflecting the crazy colors of the exploding fireworks make it a spectacular and memorable sight. Eagle Nest Lake

A storm moving in over Eagle Nest Lake.

Expansive mountain views in Eagle Nest.

dam celebrated its hundred-year anniversary in spring of 2018.

Eagle Nest Lake is technically an alpine lake since it sits at 8,300 feet elevation which makes for cool summer days great for fishing. The lake is popular with fisherman, boaters, campers, hikers, and wildlife enthusiasts. An abundance of animals makes it an ideal location for wildlife viewing.

The lake freezes in the winter and ice fishing is popular. The lake provides good fishing now, but it went through low levels and tough times for a while. You can catch brown, cutthroat, rainbow trout, and kokanee salmon, as well as lake trout (mackinaw). This lake is regularly stocked with trout and kokanee salmon. Anglers use downriggers for kokanee salmon and cowbells for trout, but if you fish early or late, you can catch trout in the shallows.

You can catch in smaller numbers smallmouth bass, yellow perch, common carp, white sucker (you may get way too many of these on your line), channel catfish, sunfish, and northern pike, which were accidentally introduced into Eagle Nest Lake. The park recommends anglers to keep the pike because of their threat to the lake's gamefish populations. The lake has a state park for camping and access with two boat ramps on the northwest side.

Near Eagle Nest you should be able to scan the vistas and spot the 13,161-foot peak towering in the distance. Snowmobiling is extremely popular in and around Eagle Nest in the winter. If you want some of the best small-stream tailwater fishing in the Southwest, go fish the Cimarron River (see page 39) that comes out of Eagle Nest Lake.

SIDE TRIP: **DISCOVER THE OLD WEST IN CIMARRON**

43

From Eagle Nest, take US 64 east for 24 miles to Cimarron. Along this stretch, the road goes up in elevation and gives you a great view of Eagle Nest Lake. Pull over in any safe place and take that photo. You'll travel through Cimarron Canyon State Park, a gorgeous twisting road, complete with cold-water stream and steep granite cliffs.

If you want to glimpse a bit of the Old West, you need to take a couple of hours and visit nearby Cimarron. This picturesque village located on the Santa Fe Trail was once a quintessential Western town with wagons and stagecoaches; saloons and gambling halls; gunfights and knife fights; outlaws such as Jesse James, Clay Allison, and Black Jack Ketchum; and was the location of the bloody Colfax County War of 1875. You'll find numerous historic sites in Old Town, including the Old Mill Museum (220 West 17th Street, Cimarron, NM 87714). Don't miss the historic St. James Hotel (617 South Collison Avenue, Cimarron, NM 87714) and the Cimarron Canyon State Park (28869 US 64, Eagle Nest, NM 87718) either.

The St. James Hotel is an historic and reputedly haunted hotel. It's still one of the best lodgings in northeast New Mexico but its history is what put it on the map. It once housed a saloon that saw its fair share of gunfights and gambling. Zane Grey wrote novels while staying in

The St. James Hotel in Cimarron, established 1872.

room 22. Lew Wallace (author of Ben Hur and first governor of New Mexico), Billy the Kid, General Sheridan, Pat Garrett, Frederick Remington, Wyatt Earp, and Buffalo Bill Cody were guests at the hotel too. And, oh yeah, the hotel is supposedly haunted. The second floor and rooms 17 and 18 in particular are the hotspots for the phantasmic activity.

The Cimarron River offers 12 miles of some of the best trout fishing in the Southwest with three thousand to four thousand catchable trout per mile. The Cimarron flows from Eagle Nest Lake through Cimarron Canyon State Park, so the tandem is close enough that you can fish and enjoy both in a single day.

The tailwater is tight water, with lots of overhanging brush and willows. By October fishing is tough because flows become low, but from spring to fall it's a fantastic getaway for both fly and spin anglers for wild brown and stocked rainbow trout. Cimarron trout enjoy bounteous and regular hatches, so fly anglers have a definite advantage.

Cimarron Canyon State Park

28869 US 64, Eagle Nest, NM 87718

(575) 377-6271

The Colin Neblett Wildlife Area is the largest state wildlife area (33,116 acres) and includes Cimarron Canyon State Park, one of the most scenic parks in the West. The Cimarron River rushes through the canyon past the steep cliffs of the Palisades. Picnic areas and campgrounds are located in the canyon. You'll see deer, elk, and other wildlife, but this is a great area to spot a bear. Be safe as you drive on the curvy 12 miles of road and watch for deer early in the day and at dusk and dark. The park has numerous campgrounds for fee-based public tent and RV camping along the river, the biggest of which is the Gravel Pit Lakes Campground (which has two small trout-filled lakes). You don't have to pay to drive through the park, but there is a small fee to park. The park offers an amazing number of pullouts and picnic areas too. You don't want to miss seeing the Palisades, a 400-foot-tall jagged granite outcrop at mile marker 292 beside the Clear Creek Trail, where a murder took place in 1875 that started the infamous Colfax County War.

The Cimarron River has two feeder streams, Clear Creek, Tolby Creek and numerous popular hiking trails, including: Jasper-Agate, Black Jack Park Trail, Maverick (New Loop), Maverick (Old Loop), Clear Creek Trail, Lower Tolby Creek Loop, Touch-Me-Not, Tolby Meadow. From Tolby Creek to Ute Park, you will find over 8 miles of two-lane winding forested canyon road running right beside the Cimarron River that flows from Eagle Nest Lake Dam. This tailwater has incredible fishing, great density of catchable trout, and is heavily trafficked, with cars, campers, hikers, and anglers.

OTHER THINGS
to See and Do from Eagle Nest to Angel Fire

WHEELER PEAK WILDERNESS

You can access Wheeler Peak Wilderness from the north by way of
NM 578 in Red River.

The Wheeler Peak Wilderness was so designated in 1964 and now has
a total of 19,180 acres. The wilderness lies along the top of the Sangre de
Cristo Mountains and is wild and high terrain, not for the faint of heart.
Elevations in Wheeler Peak Wilderness range from a low of 7,650 feet to
a high of 13,161 feet at Wheeler Peak, and with its alpine tundra is the
highest point in the state of New Mexico.

On the northern boundary is the Taos Ski Valley. At Twining Campground
Parking Lot you can access a trail system which leads into the wilderness
and to its numerous rugged peaks. Find the Wheeler Peak Trail here (see
page 143) and continue on a trail to Horseshoe Lake or follow the ridge to
Simpson Peak and Taos Cone into Sawmill Park. Wheeler Peak Wilderness
has three alpine lakes as well as forests, tundra, and glacial cirques, and is
popular year-round with recreationalists; in fact, this area has some of the
best backcountry skiing in the Southwest.

PHILMONT BOY SCOUT RANCH

17 Deer Run Road, Cimarron, NM 87714
(575) 376-2281

As the largest Boy Scout ranch in the world and located just about
10 miles south of Cimarron, Philmont is an impressive ranch of 214 square
miles (12 miles by 30 miles). It is also the National Training Center and High
Adventure Base for the Boy Scouts, and hosts nearly twenty-five thousand
Scouts, explorers, and leaders annually. The scouts enjoy horseback riding,
hiking, backpacking, fishing, and other leadership and service training. The
ranch and its museums are open to the public.

*From left to right, top: Wheeler Peak Wilderness sign in its high-rugged terrain;
the Upper Rio Hondo. Bottom: a young angler on the Cimarron River; the rustic
welcome to Philmont, the largest Boy Scout ranch in the world.*

FROM
ANGEL FIRE
TO TAOS

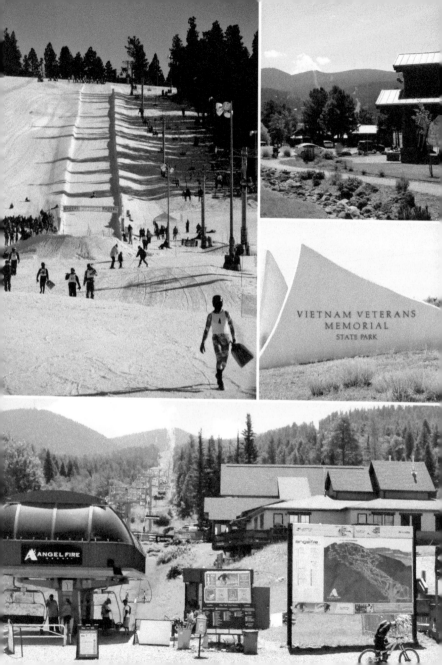

ANGEL FIRE

Route: Leave Eagle Nest on US 64 south and drive 12.6 miles to
NM 434; go south on NM 434 for 2.1 miles to Angel Fire.

Elevation: 8,406 feet

Population: 1,113

Lay of the land: valley, mountains

Angel Fire Resort was incorporated as a town in 1987 and has a
population of 1,113 Angel Fire is an uncrowded, no-frills, photogenic
little ski town, one of the last in the West to be overdeveloped and
overrun. Angel is neither, yet. The village sits in Moreno Valley at
8,400 feet surrounded by gorgeous mountains that rise up all round
to 11,000 feet, and the sentinel mountain, Wheeler Peak (13,161 feet),
watches from the northern end of the valley.

Angel Fire is about a thirty-minute drive east of Taos. The
weather is cold and snowy in winter, ideal for winter sports; in the
summer, the weather is a cool getaway from summer heat for folks
from Texas, Kansas, Oklahoma, and the hotter parts of New Mexico.
But overall, the weather is mild and the humidity low.

Because Angel Fire is a relatively young town, there is no old
mining town, town center, or main street with old brick buildings, so
it lacks the architectural and cultural charms usually associated with
ski towns. Angel Fire makes up for it with a state-of-the-art ski resort,
a laid-back, unpretentious, family-oriented, inexpensive vibe built
around seasonal activities and the beauty of the valley.

Angel Fire is a four-season destination, one of the best ski resorts
in New Mexico (second only to Taos). Angel Fire enjoys three hundred
days of sunshine annually and is significantly less expensive than
other ski towns in New Mexico and Colorado. The area was named by

*Top left: World Champion Shovel Races at Angel Fire Resort. Top right: Frontier Park
in Angel Fire. Middle right: entrance sign to Vietnam Veterans Memorial State Park.
Bottom: Summer at Angel Fire.*

Ute Indians for the fiery glow on the mountains at sunrise and sunset.

Lots of part-timers and second-homers and weekenders reside here. You'll find a mix of slope-side condos, cute cabins, and big log-cabin-style houses. Locals will tell you jokingly that at times, the elk outnumber the residents.

Transportation/Parking

Parking at Angel Fire Resort (10 Miller Lane, Angel Fire, NM 87710) is free, as are the shuttles to and from the base area during the wintertime. Shuttles run from 8:30 a.m. to 5:00 p.m. and longer for nighttime skiing days and holidays. Shuttles will also transport skiers from designated shuttle stops to the mountain for a one-dollar cash fee each way. They do offer a ten-dollar punch card worth twelve trips. The Country Club shuttle also runs from The Lodge (at the base of the mountain) to the Country Club during winter, including daily trips to the Nordic Center.

VISIT THE VIETNAM VETERANS MEMORIAL STATE PARK

44

34 Country Club Rd, Angel Fire, NM 87710
(575) 377-2293
Travel south of Eagle Nest on US 64
for 9.4 miles. The entrance is to your right.

The Vietnam Veterans Memorial, outside of Angel Fire, was the first major national memorial for Vietnam Veterans in our country. Heartbroken parents of fallen soldier Lt. David Westphall III built this tribute for their beloved son and for all who lost their lives during Vietnam. Before their son's death, the Westphall family was set to build a resort on their New Mexican property, but those plans took a turn upon hearing of their son's passing, and now their land and the memorial have become a New Mexico State Park.

It's easy to drive past this park on the way to ski or to visit another spot upon the Enchanted Circle, so put it on your itinerary.

The Vietnam Veterans Memorial along the road to Sipapu.

It's touching, moving, and many visitors need the tissues that are strategically placed about the museum and chapel to dab their tears. It's informative too. There's a section of the museum dedicated to women and their role at home and abroad during this controversial war time. There's a forty-five-minute film and several displays of memorabilia throughout the museum. For many, it's hard to quit looking at all the photographs and into the eyes of the people who were there and experienced Vietnam.

The memorial grounds include a Huey helicopter that saw action in Vietnam, an amphitheater, a memorial walk, gardens, and more. The parents of the fallen Westphall have since passed away and both of their gravesites are on the grounds of the place they built for their son and for so many others.

Today, the Vietnam Veterans Memorial State Park honors all members of America's armed forces and serves as a place of healing, learning, and reuniting. Ultimately it serves as place to pay respect and show honor to all who have served our country.

The David Westphall Veterans Foundation, established in 1988, supports a wellness and healing center for our veterans and has a goal to collect photos of all 58,261 veterans on the Wall. Thirteen photos each month are rotated into the chapel of those who lost their lives in Vietnam or are MIA. To have a photo represented at the chapel, contact the foundation at (575) 377-6900.

Visiting the museum and chapel is free, but there are plenty of ways to contribute to this touching place that honors our vets' courage and call to duty. Shop in the gift shop, volunteer, or make a donation. You can even purchase a brick with your vet's name engraved for the memorial's honorary walkway.

This is one of the most thought-provoking, touching sites around, especially here in the Moreno Valley of New Mexico along the beautiful Enchanted Circle.

SKI AT THE ANGEL FIRE RESORT

10 Miller Lane, Angel Fire, NM 87710
(575) 377-4499

45

From Eagle Nest, travel south on US 64 for about 9.4 miles and turn left (south) on NM 434. Drive 2.1 miles on NM 434 to North Angel Fire Road. Turn left on North Angel Fire Road and drive east/southeast for a little less than a mile where you'll find the main hotel and lots of parking lots.

Winter is the most popular season in Angel Fire, especially with families. There's not a lot of town around this ski resort, but there are plenty of activities to keep visitors busy and having fun. This area of New Mexico in the Sangre de Cristo Mountains averages over two hundred inches of snow each year, making many outdoor winter enthusiasts happy. In addition to the eighty-plus runs, Angel Fire has three terrain parks and four gladed tree skiing areas. The resort has also added a newly developed hike to an advanced section for extreme

Angel Fire Ski Resort is family friendly and has runs for all skill levels.

skiers. And Angel Fire Resort provides about the only nighttime skiing in New Mexico. For a reasonable fee added to your lift ticket, you'll have star-studded access to fifty acres of trails and a terrain park on the frontside of the mountain. If you just want to give this moonlit opportunity a try, you can purchase a nighttime pass only.

Nordic skiing and snowshoeing are available on over 7 miles of trails at the Country Club's Nordic Center. The center also has a sledding hill for kids age twelve and under. If you're staying at

Angel Fire Resort Stats

Average annual snowfall: 210 inches

Base elevation: 8,600 feet

Summit elevation: 10,677 feet

Vertical drop: 2,077 feet

Hours for mountain use: 9:00 a.m.–4:00 p.m.; 5:00 p.m.–8:00 p.m. for night skiing (select nights)

Number of trails: 80 total: 21% beginner, 56% intermediate, 23% advanced

Number of lifts: 2 quads, 3 doubles, 2 Sunkid Wondercarpets

Terrain parks: 3 total: Night Rider (a combination of small- and medium-sized features), Sweet Street, Beginner Park off Headin' Home (featuring beginner and intermediate rails and boxes), and Liberation Park at the Summit (includes progressive features as well as multiple jumps, rails, fun boxes for advanced riders. They also added a new boarder cross/skier cross course including high berms, sweeping turns, and small, medium, and large rollers.).

Glade skiing: 4 glades totaling 30 acres: Bear Glade, Elk Glade, Shane's Glade, and Eagle Glade. All are designated as advanced terrain.

Snowmaking capabilities: 52% of the mountain, 85% of beginner terrain
—from Angel Fire Resort, angelfireresort.com/activities/winter-activities/
skiing-and-snowboarding/mountain-stats/

The Lodge, you can catch their free shuttle to the Nordic Center and Angel Fire's slopes.

Back at Angel Fire's mountain, the five-lane Polar Coaster tubing hill allows everyone forty-two inches and taller to take their turn. Kids have to ride on their own tube. Come prepared with your own shoes, as ski boots aren't allowed on the tubing hill. You can purchase passes for an hour at a time from the Angel Fire ticket office.

Lessons are available for all kinds of skiing, from downhill and boarding to Nordic. Even a sunset, private lesson is an option. Angel Fire offers special programs for the kids including day care at Snow Bear Camp. One of the perks that parents love about Angel Fire is the option for parents to share a lift ticket, known as a parenting pass, so while one parent skis with an older child, for example, the other can stay back with the littlest one who's too young to ski, and then parents can swap places.

Fifth graders ski free with a report card; kids under age six and those age seventy-five and over ski free too. They do offer up a great deal on a family season pass, especially if you purchase it in the fall. One of the mountain's easy runs goes from the top to the bottom, making youngsters feel like the grown-ups as they get to ride the lift all the way to the top and ski all the way down. This mountain-long run is great for anyone learning or just wanting to take it easy. It's no wonder Angel Fire gets high marks from families.

There are a number of festive celebrations at the slopes, from Christmas Eve and New Year's Eve torchlight parades to January's Big Ol' Texas Weekend to February's fun-spirited shovel races and Mardi Gras Celebration, plus a little beach-like fun in March. There's something fun going on at Angel Fire all winter long.

46 RIDE THE SUMMER GONDOLA AT THE RESORT

The summer gondola is located at the
Angel Fire Resort (see page 225).

Summertime at Angel Fire brings its own kind of fun. The skies are
blue the majority of the time, everything on the ground is green and
colorful, and the temperatures feel great. So being outside is where
everyone wants to be. Even in the summertime, afternoon showers
are refreshing.

A summer lift ticket will also lead you to loads of hiking trails
throughout the mountain. Stop at the top for a bite at their mountain
restaurant or for some rounds of disc golf, free with a lift ticket and
disc package. It can also lead you to a more relaxed approach of being
out in nature by riding the lift up and back down. The ride will give you
plenty of time to soak in the views of the beautiful Moreno Valley and,

Looking for Something Different to Do in Angel Fire?

- Take photos at the Balloons Over Angel Fire festival
  (angelfireresort.com/event/balloons-over-angel-fire/) in June.
- Go to the Farmers' Market (3367 NM 434, Angel Fire, NM 87710)
  on Sundays in the summer to buy homemade goods, or art, or
  produce, or...
- Fish and paddle board on Monte Verde Lake (rentals available).
- Go on a gold-panning expedition or sleigh ride with a local outfitter.
- Get in on early-bird first tracks on the snow-covered slopes.
- Ski with a guide and take a mountain tour (look for guides in
  bright yellow jackets).
- Attend the summer music festival (angelfireresort.com/event/
  music-angel-fire-summer-festival/).
- Ride the summertime zipline at the ski resort.

The chairlift at Angel Fire Bike Park helps bikers reach the best trails.

if the sky is clear, spot New Mexico's famed Wheeler Peak and Eagle Nest Lake. All lift tickets are reasonably priced and worth their fee.

Off mountain, head to the Country Club (100 Country Club Drive, Angel Fire, NM 87710, (575) 377-3055) for golfing at their picturesque seventy-two-par course. Book your tee time at least a week in advance to ensure your spot on these greens, lined with aspen and evergreens, with smaller greens and bunkers on the back nine. Tennis and pickleball players can get in some play at the Angel Fire Resort Tennis Center; just register at the Country Club. Rentals and lessons are available.

HIT THE TRAILS AT ANGEL FIRE BIKE PARK

47

The bike park is located at the Angel Fire Resort (see page 225).

Mountain bikers flock to Angel Fire for its award-winning bike park, the largest in the Rockies and known as one of the best of its kind in the southwest. The on-mountain park has over 60 miles of purpose-built, lift-served bike terrain covering 2,000 vertical feet. Trails are for all skill levels, but the park is a draw for the extreme, speed-loving, downhill riders. Our nephew-in-law owns a bike shop in Amarillo and goes here often, and he says that Angel Fire Bike Park is one of the top parks in the Southwest. Overall, mountain biking isn't for the faint of heart, so wear a helmet, inspect your equipment ahead of time, and take all precautions. Angel Fire will rent everything you need for your ride. All riders age seventeen and under will need a parent to sign a waiver. Don't fret if you're a newbie. The staff here offer group or personalized lessons on the bike park. Otherwise, grab your lift ticket and hit the trails.

Hikes around Angel Fire

ANGEL FIRE SKI AREA

Distance: 8.4 miles

Elevation gain: 2,250 feet

Trailhead: Follow North Angel Fire Road until it ends and park in the lot next to the ski school.

Hike up trail left of the lift then follow ski trails to summit. There is also a short, half-mile loop near the summit.

MONTE VERDE LAKE TRAIL:

Distance: 1 to 3.5 miles

Elevation gain: None

Trailhead: From Angel Fire, take NM 434 south for 3 miles to the parking lot of Monte Verde Lake.

This trail is easy, ideal for beginning hikers, little hikers, or those who just want to get outside and do something. If you want the 1-mile hike, go around the lake with a small detour to avoid a marshy area near the south end of the lake. To extend the hike, go south from Monte Verde Lake on Alpine Lake Way to the trailhead for Lady Slipper Trail.

TRAVEL THE PALO FLECHADO PASS

48

The Palo Flechado Pass begins 18 miles east of Taos and 12.7 miles west/southwest of Eagle Nest on your way back to Taos. From Angel Fire, head north on Mountain View Boulevard to reach US 64 west to reach the pass.

Palo Flechado Pass is a nice stopping point on the drive from Angel Fire to Taos. This pass was used as early as the 1700s by Native Americans (Kiowa, Apache and Comanche), Europeans, and Spaniards to go to and from Taos from the eastern plains. Palo Flechado Pass has also been known as Taos Pass and Old Taos Pass over the years.

In English, Palo means "stick" or "tree," while La Flecha means "arrow" and was the original name of the Cimarron River. You'll note that the historic marker suggests that the name for the pass, a tree pierced with arrows, came from two different origins: 1) The band of Apaches who frequented the area and traversed the pass were called "the Flecha de Palo", and 2) the Taos Pueblo Indians had a tradition of shooting an arrow in a tree after a fruitful buffalo hunt. Either way, it's hard to visit the pass

The Palo Flechado Pass was popular with Native Americans, Spanish, and Anglos.

without imagining the frontiersmen and Native Americans using this forested thoroughfare.

Even today you won't find any services and few houses on this entire stretch. This pass is also the boundary for Colfax and Taos Counties. Once you descend Palo Flechado Pass, don't ride your brakes or by the time you get near the bottom, you may have burnt your brakes to the point of no return. Think about using a lower gear and coast through turns. You'll enter into the canyon of the Rio Fernando de Taos. There are picnic areas, campsites, and many trails through the canyon. You'll pass by the Valle Escondido and Shady Brook communities. Taos Canyon is home to many artist studios which are open to visitors much of the summer and fall season.

SIDE TRIP: **VACATION AT THE SIPAPU SKI AND SUMMER RESORT**

5224 NM-518, Vadito, NM 87579
(800) 587-2240
This laid-back getaway is located just 24 miles southeast of Taos on NM 518 and only two hours north of Albuquerque. From Angel Fire, drive back to Taos on US 64 west, then follow NM 68 south; head south on NM 518 for 20 miles until you reach the resort.

This year-round small mountain resort (8,200 feet elevation) was founded in 1952. Located on the Rio Pueblo, Sipapu (which means "land of paradise" or "spirit place") is a low-key, family-oriented resort. The prices are some of the lowest for skiing in New Mexico. The resort is nestled in the Carson National Forest and there are no frills here, no fancy hotels, just a small manageable, uncrowded, inexpensive getaway. The resort has undergone renovation since an unfortunate fire in 2016. It now offers a 2,141-square-foot addition at the base area with rental shop, locker room, and more. It's also adding over thirty rooms to its lodging facility.

Sipapu continues a long-standing tradition of being the first

On the road to Sipapu, on the banks of the Rio del Pueblo

ski resort to open in the state, thanks to its on-point snowmaking combined with their 190 inches of annual snowfall. Sipapu is also noted as having the longest ski season in the state, keeping skiers and boarders happy into April.

Sipapu may appear as a little spot on the road, but it's so much more. It's about family, friendliness, and having fun. Sipapu even has four terrain parks for those who want to catch some air with a breakdown of trails as such: 20 percent beginner, 40 percent intermediate, 25 percent advanced, 15 percent expert

Summertime at Sipapu makes for a perfect vacation spot. It's right on the Rio Pueblo, which flows through the resort, and there's a stocked trout-fishing pond. Try your hand at fishing, or sit back and relax by these cool mountain waters. There's also disc golf, hiking, geocaching, camping, and more. Check out Sipapu's special events, competitions, and good deals throughout the year (like special deals on free lift tickets and free lodging) at sipapunm.com/.

50 SIDE TRIP: **EXPLORE LAS VEGAS, NEW MEXICO**

City of Las Vegas Visitor Center, 500 Railroad Avenue, Las Vegas, NM 87701
(505) 425-3707
From Angel Fire, take NM 434 south to Mora, then NM 518 south to Las Vegas.

This gem is rapidly becoming one of our favorites in the state. Las Vegas has reestablished itself as a major force in northern New Mexico after having fulfilled that role more than a hundred years ago. The growing town right off of I-25 has a thriving artist's community and a university and a college. It is located nearby to both Taos and Santa Fe and the major east-west interstate I-40.

The centerpieces of Las Vegas are the Old Town Historic District and the famous Plaza Hotel. The Plaza Hotel was called "The Belle of the Southwest" when it was built in 1882 and has since been beautifully renovated. The hotel is gorgeous and holds watch over the Old Town Plaza. Like so many historic hotels in the Southwest, many celebrities have stayed on the premises and there are stories of ghosts haunting the place. The hotel is listed on the National Register of Historic Places and has been the setting for many movies and television shows including *Longmire* and *No Country for Old Men*. The town of Las Vegas has also been the filming location for numerous movies over the years including *Easy Rider*, *Red Dawn*, and *All the Pretty Horses*, to name a few.

The Old Town area has many small hometown shops, antiques, bookstores, coffee shops, etc. It offers big-city amenities in a small, friendly town. There two National Forests within minutes of

The Historic Plaza Hotel is a nineteenth-century charmer that sits in the Old Town Historic District.

downtown Las Vegas, and you may also enjoy visiting one of the many campgrounds along the Gallinas River. Storrie Lake State Park is only 5 miles from town.

OTHER THINGS
to See and Do from Angel Fire to Taos

SIDE TRIP: MORA

From Angel Fire take NM 434 south toward Mora, a 34-mile drive. The canyon road is twisty and narrow with several stream crossings. You'll pass Coyote Creek State Park (17 miles), and after that the road runs through bottom of the valley with its old Spanish-heritage farmlands.

The tiny, historic village of Mora is a good place to gas up, see what small town New Mexico is like, and head back to Angel Fire. Two family-friendly places to visit include the Salman Raspberry Ranch (from Las Vegas, go north on NM 518 for 25 miles, then turn right at the Salman Ranch sign onto NM 442; (575) 387-2900), one of the largest purveyors of raspberries in northern New Mexico, and the Victory Alpaca Ranch (MM1 NM 434, Mora, NM 87732; (575) 387-2254), where you can touch and feed alpacas.

HIKING THE ELLIOT BARKER TRAIL

From Angel Fire, travel south on US 64 5.3 miles. If coming from Taos, take US 64 (Kit Carson Street) east from the plaza. Just after mile marker 274, turn right into the parking area at the trailhead.

Hike the Elliot Barker Trail (8,500 feet in elevation) for beautiful views of Angel Fire and Wheeler Peak Wilderness. This is an all-season trail for hikers, mountain bikers, horseback riders, cross country skiers, snowshoers, and snowmobilers.

There are a number of trail choices along

The Elliot Barker Trail is a popular, moderate hike with lots of connecting trails.

Elliot Barker. And since the trail is part of the Adopt-A-Trail system between the local trekkers club and the National Forest Service it has the benefit of continued development and expansion. An easy, short option is to take the short quarter-mile-plus trek to the pond for a picnic. For more, continue from the pond to explore the longer Palo Flechado Pass Loop Trail of about 5.5 miles and gaining 1,000 feet in elevation. Or, before reaching the pond, take a left when you come to a primitive fence about a quarter of a mile in and take the left trail of the fork for a 1.5-mile-loop hike back to the trailhead. Or, take the right fork and make the trek to the trail's peak elevation of 9,300 feet to Apache Pass.

Other options include the Bull Spring and Apache Pass Extension Tail and the Woop De Do Extension Trail, which has a few woop-de-do jumps for mountain bikers.

The trail system utilizes old logging roads and animal paths and overall receives a moderate rating. Elliot Barker trails will take you through a forest of fir, spruce, and aspen and a jaunt through high-mountain meadows, which in springtime can be filled with colorful wildflowers. Study the US Forest Service map (fs.usda.gov/Internet/FSE_MEDIA/stelprdb5339096.pdf) for the path that best suits your needs as well as the Elliot Barker sign at the trailhead for options and estimated distances of the trails. (Hint: take a photo of the sign for easy access along the way.) As with any hike, be prepared with water and other provisions and keep an eye out for wildlife.

Leaving Elliot Barker Trail on US 64, this high-elevation winding road between Angel Fire and Taos is one of the most gorgeous stretches of the circle trip, with grand views, mountains peeking out from green forests, and twisty narrow turns. The road can be treacherous in winter at times. Watch for bicyclists and don't crowd them because you need to share the road and some of these drop-offs are steep. You will see several pullouts for photos, and to let that fast driver get around you. The scenery is among the most jaw dropping of the entire Enchanted Circle. You'll come to Palo Flechado Pass a little more than 2 miles after Elliot Barker Trail and it's worth pulling over (several places to park) and taking some pics.

Fall Foliage in New Mexico

Fall brings about a brilliant transformation to the New Mexican landscape. The foliage changes color and the high-altitude aspen trees begin to quake their golden leaves. The Enchanted Circle has several opportunities for leaf peeping, which you can see from the road as well as nestled along its hidden trails. A couple of trails with aspen groves include the Columbine Trail (see page 163) between Questa and Red River and the Goose Creek Trail (see page 197; it's 6 miles to the lake, but you don't have to go that far). Not up to hiking? Check out horseback riding trips in Red River at redriver.org/things-to-do/summer-recreation/horseback-riding.

Angel Fire has a chairlift ride (located at the Angel Fire Resort at 10 Miller Lane, Angel Fire, NM 87710; call (575) 377-4320 for more information) for an easygoing way to experience a colorful New Mexican fall. It's impossible to say the exact week the colors peak, but it's usually somewhere from mid- to end of September to early October. But this depends on many factors, including the weather and altitude as well as sunlight and soil moisture. Weather makes a big difference as to when we will start to notice all the vibrant fall colors. If your plans are flexible, call the Angel Fire Visitor Center at (575) 377-6555 for updates on color changes, and when they say it's a go, pack your bags and get here because the leaves don't last long.

A few other choice places to view the brilliant oranges, reds, golds, and yellows of autumn include:

- The drive from Tres Piedras to Tierra Amarilla. You want wilderness? No homes? Big country, lots of forest, photo opportunities? This 49-mile drive has it all. Lots of pullouts, but no stores nor gas stations.
- Angel Fire to Taos Canyon
- High Road from Taos to Santa Fe
- Chairlift rides at Red River and Taos Ski Valley
- NM 518 south from Taos to Sipapu
- Almost any high-country hike

Top: beautiful mountain view near Questa. Bottom left: fall foliage along the Red River. Middle right: fishing pond in Red River. Bottom right: the road through Cimarron Canyon.

INDEX

Page locators in *italics* indicate photographs.

CPSIA information can be obtained
at www.ICGtesting.com
Printed in the USA
BVHW09s1048270818
525375BV00001B/1/P